COMPUTER SCIENCE, TECHNOLOGY AND APPLICATIONS

COMPUTERS IN EDUCATION

TRENDS, APPLICATIONS AND CHALLENGES

COMPUTER SCIENCE, TECHNOLOGY AND APPLICATIONS

Additional books and e-books in this series can be found on Nova's website under the Series tab.

EDUCATION IN A COMPETITIVE AND GLOBALIZING WORLD

Additional books and e-books in this series can be found on Nova's website under the Series tab.

Table 1. Major responses of the government, local municipalities, and schools

Month	Events
January	16th First novel coronavirus patient was confirmed in Japan. 30th First novel coronavirus task force meeting took place.
February	13th Japanese government announced the first shot against the coronavirus, consisting of 15.3 billion Japanese yen. 19th Passengers with negative test results started to go ashore from the cruise ship, Diamond Princess. 25th The Japanese government announced key principles for provisions against the coronavirus infection. 27th Prime Minister Shinzo Abe requested schools all over Japan (elementary schools, high schools and special needs schools) to call off classes from 2nd March.
March	2nd Following the governmental request, 99% of schools started closing. 10th A Revision of the Act on Special Measures for Pandemic Influenza and New Infectious Diseases Preparedness and Response was approved by the cabinet. 24th Prime Minister Abe and the International Olympic Committee (IOC) agreed to postpone the Olympics and Paralympics until 2021. 24th MEXT requested that schools restart with appropriate measures against the coronavirus. 25th The Tokyo Municipal Government requested a voluntary ban against leaving home.
April	5th The amount of infected patients exceeded 1,000 in Tokyo. 7th Prime Minister Abe declared a state of emergency based on the Act on Special Measures for Pandemic Influenza and New Infectious Diseases Preparedness and Response intended for Tokyo, Saitama, Chiba, Kanagawa, Osaka, Hyogo, and Fukuoka lasting until 6th May. 9th The amount of infected patients exceeded 5,000, excluding those on the cruise ship. 16th Prime Minister Abe declared a state of emergency across the country. 29th Prime Minister Abe expressed interest in the idea of fall admissions.
May	1st MEXT notified the educational boards in local governments to prioritize first, sixth, and nine graders once schools restarted. 4th Prime Minister Abe announced the extension of the state of emergency, addressing a "new way of life" in the protracted fight against the coronavirus. 14th The state of emergency was lifted in 39 prefectures, excluding eight prefectural and city governments (Hokkaido, Tokyo, Kanagawa, Saitama, Chiba, Osaka, Kyoto, and Hyogo). 21st The state of emergency was lifted in Kyoto, Osaka, and Hyogo. 22nd Tokyo Metropolitan Governor, Yuriko Koike, released a roadmap as an exit strategy for Tokyo, looking ahead to construct a society where the "new way of life" would prevail. 25th The state of emergency was lifted all over Japan. 29th Minister from MEXT said not to form a hasty conclusion regarding fall admissions.

According to a survey conducted by the Ministry of Education, Culture, Sports, Science and Technology in Japan (hereinafter MEXT), 99% of public schools (elementary, lower secondary, upper secondary schools and special needs education schools) which were closed due to coronavirus restarted as of the first of June (MEXT 2020c). Among these, 55% restarted their education program following a regular timetable. This was a long-awaited recommencement; however, it also marks the beginning of starting to explore a “new way of life” in schools. Schools are taking measures including staggering students’ attendance, regular disinfection and better air ventilation, and spacing of seats and desks. Education boards, schools, and teachers are in the midst of exploring new ways of teaching. Furthermore, operational policies regarding club activities, gatherings, and school events will also come under pressure to be reviewed. Nearly all sports and cultural events have been cancelled. Some municipalities planned to shorten the summer break (usually almost the full month of August) to make up for lost time.

The major responses to coronavirus by the Japanese central and local governments and schools are summarized in Table 1.

Measures Taken by MEXT

During the school closures, MEXT requested that local municipalities make maximum efforts to utilize information and communications technology (ICT) at every opportunity to guarantee children's chances of learning. They stressed the use of online teaching with teleconference systems and online teaching materials, using handouts and TV broadcasts for different purposes (MEXT 2020d, 2020e). In addition to this, MEXT set up a dedicated website to support students’ study at home (MEXT online1). Moreover, MEXT is trying to promote the use of ICT in education in local governments at the moment. MEXT launched the GIGA (Global and Innovation Gateway for All) school initiative in 2019, which aimed to achieve an ICT-based individualized and optimized learning environment by distributing one laptop per child by the 2023 fiscal year secondary schools in the Tokyo metropolitan area restarted teaching online in April. However, the impact on the whole of the education system in Japan seems to be limited as the ratio in elementary, lower secondary, and upper secondary schools is not much more than 6%. It does not mean that all private schools can guarantee the opportunity to learn during school closures, however, there is a concern that the gap is widening between those who have access to quality education and those who do not during this period.

Grassroot Movements by Parents

Meanwhile, some parents have lasting concerns about the support provided by schools during the school closures, which meant that each household had to provide education. There is a movement of parents and guardians which wants to influence local government as they cannot bear to see the lackluster response of municipalities and schools. Volunteer parents who have elementary and/or lower secondary school children in Musashino city, Tokyo, conducted a survey on online learning among parents and collected 1,555 answers (Voluntary group of Musashino city online). As a result, 96.1% of parents who have elementary school pupils and 96.8% who have lower secondary pupils agreed with online learning. Arguments for online learning included "I am worried that the education schedule could become overloaded when school restarts to catch up with pupils' studies. I expect online learning to be a chance to communicate with other pupils and teachers even during the school closures," and "I print out free-of-charge learning materials and give them as homework to my kid, but he gets bored with them and it is hard to continue studying at home every day." Arguments against online learning included, even though they were in the minority, "not all households are equipped with a network. We don't have a computer, a tablet, or a PC, which would be necessary for online learning," and "I prefer face-to-face instruction at school by commuting, rather than online learning." Opinions varied in terms of how to support the network environment at home: 29.5% thought a tablet or PC should be distributed to all households, 54.8% thought a tablet or PC should be distributed to households which needed it, and 13.8% thought a dedicated place should be prepared at school (1403 answers from parents with elementary school pupils). Issues such as these regarding fairness and equality are exactly what local governments must address when they put plans into action. Based on the results, the parental group is requesting a chance to have a meeting with those in charge of the city.

Another parental group in Tokyo summarized the actual situation regarding online learning in each ward in Tokyo, collecting information from parents who have school-aged children, under the slogan "do not stop learning" (Papamamastartup 2020). This grassroots activity categorized 23 wards into "top" groups and a group which had "started to run," hoping to work on the local governments, some of which remain slow in implementing online learning. The results showed that even in Tokyo, one of the most seemingly advanced regions in Japan, the extent of efforts vary widely from those which have adopted cloud applications (e.g., Microsoft Teams, Zoom, G suite for Edu, eboard), online teaching materials (e.g., e Library), and educational videos (e.g., StudySapuri), to those which do almost nothing but paper-based instruction.

Children's Daily Lives During the School Closures

In the meantime, how have children spent their time during the school closures? An emergency survey conducted mainly among elementary and upper secondary school pupils in March 2020 by Save the Children Japan presented the real picture of the situation children are in.

Regarding daily life, 14.5% spent time alone at home and 9.9% felt bored. In terms of anxiety, 31.4% could not live their normal daily life or could not go out (20.5% missed someone), 16.0% worried about their physical condition, spiritual change, and infection spread, and 15.7% could not study or worried about a decline in their academic ability. Regarding the coronavirus, 15.6% worried about the measures taken against the infection, and 13.0% worried about school life (Save the Children Japan 2020).

In addition to this, children were emotionally and physically stressed due to the cancellation of or simplified graduation ceremonies, the temporary standstill of club activities, and isolation due to not seeing friends or significant others, all because of the sudden decision to close schools. Small children tended not to understand the situation. The report also gave a glimpse into signs of threats, such as Internet and/or game addiction due to prolonged time spent at home. Additionally, upper secondary students who plan to take college entrance examinations feel anxious because of the above-mentioned confusion regarding these examinations. In summary, the report finds that Japan has not fulfilled its obligation to explain the situation to children, referring to the declaration by The Committee on the Rights of the Child (CRC), and warns of the grave physical, emotional, and psychological effects of the coronavirus pandemic on children (OHCHR 2020).

Studying at Home with a Smartphone

Next, how have children been learning at home during the school closures? As mentioned earlier, ICT is underused in schools in Japan. A study indicates a similar tendency in students' computer use at home. According to PISA 2018, the ratio of Japanese students who mentioned "doing homework on a computer" and "using learning apps or learning websites on a computer" was the worst among the participating OECD affiliated countries. Those who answered "never or hardly ever" reached as much as 78.8% for both questions. In contrast, the ratio of those who were "playing one-player games" and "chatting online" was largest among the OECD countries and the ratio of those who were "playing collaborative online games" and "playing online games via social networks" was greater than the OECD average (NIER 2018a). The results show that Japanese students use ICT more for things other than study. These are rather worrying results, but the story does not end here. It has been pointed out that inexperience in ICT even affects students' proficiency in reading. The decline of proficiency in reading in PISA 2018 (from eighth place in the ranking in 2015 to 15th in 2018) was partially or largely considered to be due to students' unfamiliarity with computer-based tests and digital texts. If this is true and continues, students' proficiency in reading, and eventually their academic performance, will be affected to a greater or lesser extent (NIER 2019).

A study conducted between April and May revealed the gap between the ideal and reality in terms of children's study at home. Only 3.7% of elementary school pupils and 6.8% of lower secondary school pupils said that they could access real-time online learning with their teachers, even though 72.8% of elementary school pupils and 63.1% of lower secondary school pupils wanted to (Asahi gakusei shimbun sha 2020). They tended to worry more about not seeing their friends and missing exercise than having delays in their studies. Parents were worried about being unprepared for online learning and not knowing when school would recommence, however, some pupils regarded the school closures as a good opportunity and said that they could learn at their own pace, take the opportunity to learn things in more depth, or even have more conversations with their families.

How do students access educational resources at home during the school closures? Apparently, smartphones are more used than computers (laptops or desktops) among students studying at home. Apps aiming to support study have been released by emerging EdTech companies and spin-off separate companies from relatively big IT firms. A study conducted in 2018 showed that 87.9% of upper secondary students said that they have studied using a smartphone (Studyplus 2018). The most popular apps for study were YouTube (43.8%), followed by Study Sapuri (educational video service) (23.2%), and Studyplus (learning history management app) (20.4%). The use of smartphones and study apps proliferated among upper secondary pupils. The study also showed that most parents (62.1%) agreed with the use of smartphones for their children's studies.

According to Nikkei Shimbun, as reported on 1st June 2020, Surala Net, a cloud-based education firm, started to provide digital learning material free-of-charge for elementary, lower secondary, and upper secondary students whose schools were closed. It covered 360 schools and 150,000 students across Japan. Digital Knowledge, a new entrant in e-learning firms, opened online courses in Math and English free-of-charge for lower secondary pupils, using the cloud-based online conferencing system, Zoom (Resemom 2020). Similar services and educational apps opened one after another regardless of whether or not payment was required. Various EdTech firms have engaged in fierce competition taking the school closures as an opportunity.

Studying using a smartphone seems perfectly suited to study at home, however, the previous study showed that parents also have concerns about difficulties regarding motivation to study, concluding that controlling motivation will be key in such educational apps and services (Studyplus 2018). Indeed, the use of a free communication application called LINE rose drastically after the nationwide school closures. The use of video chat through smartphone cameras grew more than 30% across all generations on average from March to April 2020 (LINE Corporation 2020). Meanwhile, it grew more than 80% among 10–year-olds in the same period (ibid.). LINE predicts that the trend will continue for a while. In addition, Japanese students' Internet use has been on the increase. A total of 99.1% of high schoolers use the Internet for more than four hours a day on average (Cabinet Office 2020). Against that background, the educational effects of self-study can be wiped out. A study of Tohoku university and Sendai city conducted among 24,000 lower secondary pupils showed that the longer they use a smartphone, the less their academic achievement, regardless of how many hours they study. The use of games and computers showed similar results, so the researchers recommend using them for an hour a day at most (Sendai city online).

RESPONSE FROM *JUKU* COMPANIES

Organizations having a presence in online education are *juku*, which can be translated as private tutoring school or cram school. Sports, art, or music are popular after-school activities but they are not usually known as *juku*. *Juku* are consistently used for studying major subjects and are sometimes called *gakushu-juku* (*juku* for studying). *Juku* have often been regarded as a symbol of "cold meritocracy," being characterized as endless re-teaching and drills, involved in the lucrative business of after-school schools, and competition for the "right" college (Pattersen 1993). To varying degrees, this might be true even today because one of the main reasons to go to *juku* is to gain entrance to the "right" college. The entrance examinations to colleges have not changed very much for decades. *Juku* have gained less attention of researchers. Lowe (2015) suggested that it is because researchers do not work in *juku*, they are difficult to access, and are designed only for exam preparation. In addition to this, the author believes that there may be other reasons such as the cautious attitude toward sharing know-how as a consequence of being in a competitive business industry and criticism of being part of this excessive competition. In this article, the author examines the delivery methods of the *juku* educational materials, which have been accumulated over a year of practice.

Before that, I would like to briefly review *juku* in Japan, especially their types, features, and the industrious aspect. The *juku* industry in Japan is worth approximately 957 billion Japanese yen as of 2016. This surpasses that of other developed countries. The number of *juku* totals 47,570 (METI 2017), which is more than the total of the number of elementary schools (19,738), lower secondary schools (10,222), and upper secondary schools (4,887) all over Japan (MEXT 2019). The private education industry in Japan remains big and it is a commercial enterprise with high profitability, however, it has tended to shrink due to the decline in the number of children and the number of business proprietors is declining (METI 2018).

According to a survey conducted by Benesse, one of the biggest educational service providers, the ratio of pupils going to *juku* is 49.1% for elementary school pupils, 57.0% for lower secondary pupils, and 36.3% for upper secondary pupils (Benesse 2017). (These numbers do not include activities regarding sports, art, and music.) The ratio surpasses 50% in the fourth grade in elementary school and peaks during the third year of lower secondary school. The study analyzes the reasons for the low ratio among upper secondary pupils and suggests that it results from upper secondary schools' dedicated mentoring for entrance examinations to college (ibid.). These numbers are not necessarily high when comparing the ratio of fifth graders to those in other Asian cities such as 72.9% in Seoul and 76.6% in Beijing, while it is only 51.6% in Tokyo. But even so, this shows the high level of interest in education among Japanese households (Benesse 2007).

Types of *juku* vary from specializing in one subject to teaching all the major subjects (Japanese, e.g., Contemporary Japanese language and Classics, Math, English, Science, e.g., Physics and Chemistry, and Society, e.g., World history and Japanese history), and from individual teaching to group teaching. The size also varies from one-man operations to a nationwide scale. There are various instructors from part-time undergraduate students to nationally well-known "stars" who can earn $400,000 salaries (Pattersen, 1993). The high ratio of part-time undergraduate students among instructors occasionally raises suspicion about the educational quality.

Online Education Provided by *Juku*

Given the prolonged school closures, *juku* companies have reacted in different ways, making use of their long-held teaching methods. Major *juku* companies have previously developed online lessons in various forms. In the study I referred to previously, those who had access to real-time online teaching provided by *juku* was 36.9% among elementary school pupils and 36.0% among lower secondary school pupils, while that provided by school was 3.7% and 6.8% respectively (Asahi gakusei shimbun sha 2020). Here I would like to highlight some cases of *juku* providing online education.

Nagase, one of the giant companies in the *juku* industry provided "online courses at home" free-of-charge to high school students all over Japan until the end of May 2020. Students could take two out of five subjects (English, Math, Japanese, Science, and Society) in five lots of 90–minute sessions, which were taught by various teachers including Mr. Osamu Hayashi, a nationally known star teacher in Japanese. At the end of every session, a confirmation test is available to proceed to the next session so that students can have a better grasp of what they learned (ReseMom Biz 2020). The company opened online courses even to non-member elementary and lower secondary pupils for one year, collaborating with another major *juku* firm, Yotshuya Otsuka (Toshin online). Surprisingly, it also opened its online courses to schoolteachers and education boards so that teachers in the regular education system can learn online teaching methods from *juku* instructors. This tells us that the leading role in education is no longer limited to schoolteachers and the regular school system. This, as I will discuss later, also raises questions about the roles of schools and teachers and the new way of teaching.

Sundai yobigakko closes its face-to-face courses in mid-July, and instead delivers recorded videos of classes online. Students can watch and listen to the teaching material on a PC or a smartphone. The online chat system allows students to ask questions online. In addition, the school started to provide learning materials in English, Math, Physics, and Chemistry, which have been developed by an educational AI firm, Atamaplus. With the learning material, an "AI learning coach," which has acquired coaching skills, understands the learning conditions of each student remotely and supports each student's learning through chatting online (Sundai online). As just described, *juku* has long been playing a prominent role, and given the perceived insufficient study support by the schools during the closures, it is anticipated that *juku* will step up its presence further.

FUTURE CHALLENGES

Before concluding, I would like to share three concerns stemming from the discussion so far. These are not a conclusion, but rather a presentation of the problems which should be discussed or addressed from now.

New Fairness and Equality Challenges

Education in Japan has achieved a measure of legitimacy in general, however, there is room for improvement in terms of fairness and equality. As described earlier, disparities are definitely emerging between those who have access to quality online education and those who do not. In relation to this, child poverty remains a big issue. A study conducted by UNICEF placed Japan as 27th out of 35 economically advanced countries and its poverty rate is 14.9% (UNICEF 2012). This could have worsened due to the deteriorating economy as a result of the pandemic, which needs to be kept under review.

In addition to this, the digital divide will become stronger as new fairness and equality challenges present themselves in education. Of course, this has been identified as a problem before, however, the digital divide, as is defined here, is not only about the presence or absence of a computer or a smartphone. Indeed, the ratios of upper secondary students using the Internet and smartphones were already considerably high at 99.0% and 97.5% respectively as of 2019 (Cabinet Office 2019). What makes the digital divide more complicated today is that even those who have a smartphone with Internet access can be divided into those who can use it for study and those who use it for something other than study. With no concern for the type of digital device (e.g., laptop computer or tablet PC), the same applies to the devices MEXT is planning to distribute. Digital devices would enhance the learning of already capable students and many others, which is a welcome result. However, it would also hinder those who are inexperienced with new digital devices or those who do not know how to study with them. Needless to say, the introduction of new technology itself does not solve the problem automatically, but steady and caring education does.

Reconsidering the Roles of Schools and Teachers

If digital technologies are introduced into schools now, it would break open the doors of conservative schools, and release teachers from ineffective school procedures and students from rote memory work. Or, it could even change traditional teaching methods such as textbook- and paper-based instruction, in which up to 40 students study the same subject in the same way simultaneously. This could lead to the "informatization of education" that MEXT has been aiming for. So, how will the roles of schools and teachers change? In fact, some municipalities have already decided to distribute the ID of private educational cloud services to students, in which no schoolteacher is technically needed. In some elementary schools, robots equipped with artificial intelligence are teaching pupils English on a trial basis as English became a compulsory subject for fifth and sixth graders from 2020, as reported by Kyodo news on 22nd October 2018. In the classroom where robots are teaching, do human teachers become mere staff members known as "facilitators" who support the robots? However, it is unknown if and to what extent these kinds of robots, AI, or educational cloud services will become common in schools in Japan, and whether these technologies will help teachers, or will teachers be helping them? If teaching is not an exclusive feature of teachers, what will the expertise of the teacher be? This question is not at all meant to criticize teachers. Everyone has recognized the significance of schools and teachers through school closures during this recent period. Even if the role of teaching is partially given over to computers, robots, AI, or whatever, essential elements should remain, e.g., caring, protecting, nurturing, and watching over children, which cannot be easily achieved by technology. These might be issues that lie ahead, however, the roles of schools and teachers should be reconsidered.

Addressing Individualization and Isolation

During the school closures, each student's pace of self-instruction differed greatly. Even after schools have resumed, the gap in the learning of each student should be attended to for a while. Online education will still be needed because school life is not fully back to normal. School life will not be the same as before the pandemic even after schools have resumed, e.g., children will not spend much time discussing in class, school time will be limited, and school life will be substantially restricted. Ideally, self-paced self-instruction is good in terms of avoiding *ochikobore* (dropout students) and *ukikobore* (literally meaning "floating," referring to high-achieving students who are not motivated in class). However, this is true only when there is generous teaching assistance. The way things stand, students are more and more individualized and isolated in drill-based or on-demand instruction, even if online education were fully achieved or if school life were fully back to normal. Individual students should be cared for to avoid isolation. At the same time, teachers and students will also be required to change their mindset to the "new way of life" of school as they have become familiar with group teaching for a long time.

CONCLUSION

In this article, the author reviewed a wide range of events and issues regarding school closures in Japan due to the pandemic of the novel coronavirus. Writing this article made me think that it is almost impossible to make study supported by ICT succeed without knowing and interpreting the circumstances surrounding laws, central and local governments, schools, and children. In particular, listening to and understanding what problems children are having, which has not yet been fully studied, matters in situations like this. Directing our attention to the care of children, including their socioeconomic and mental wellbeing, not only affects their learning and learning efficiency, but is of increasing significance. Given this background, I would like to stress the need for further research to discuss what kind of educational system will be needed in the future. I hope that the current situation is a suitable opportunity for a new and good education.

REFERENCES

Asahi gakusei shimbun sha. 2020. *Daily living during the school closure (in Japanese).* Accessed June 10, 2020. https://prtimes.jp/a/?f=d21716-20200522-1261.pdf.

Benesse. 2017. *Study on out-of-school educational activities in 2017(in Japanese).* Accessed June 10, 2020. https://berd.benesse.jp/up_images/research/2017_Gakko_gai_tyosa_web.pdf.

Benesse. 2007. *Basic Research on Academic Performance: International Survey of Six Cities.* Accessed June 10, 2020. https://berd.benesse.jp/berd/center/open/report/gakukihon_6toshi/soku/pdf/6toshi_english.pdf.

Cabinet Office. 2020. *Report of survey on young people's internet use (in Japanese).* Accessed June 10, 2020. https://www8.cao.go.jp/youth/youth-harm/chousa/net-jittai_list.html.

Cabinet Office. 2019. *Result of the survey on youngsters' internet usage (in Japanese).* Accessed June 10, 2020. https://www8.cao.go.jp/youth/youth-harm/chousa/h30/net-jittai/pdf/sokuhou.pdf.

Japanese Educational Research Association. 2020. *Recommendations for fall admissions (in Japanese).* Accessed June 10, 2020. http://www.jera.jp/wp-content/uploads/2020/05/JERA20200522SpecialCommitteeSummary.pdf.

LINE Corporation. 2020. *LINE usage report (in Japanese).* Accessed June 10, 2020. https://linecorp.com/ja/pr/news/ja/2020/3174.

Lowe, Robert J. 2015. *Cram Schools in Japan: The Need for Research. The Language Teacher Online*, 39(1): 26-31.

METI. 2018. *Actual state of education industry (in Japanese).* Accessed June 10, 2020. https://www.meti.go.jp/committee/kenkyukai/mirainokyositu/pdf/001_03_03.pdf.

METI. 2017. *Actual condition survey on service industry in 2017 (in Japanese).* Accessed June 10, 2020. https://www.meti.go.jp/statistics/tyo/tokusabizi/result-2/h29/pdf/h29outline.pdf.

MEXT. 2020a *Status of school closure (in Japanese).* Accessed June 10, 2020. https://www.mext.go.jp/content/20200513-mxt_kouhou02-000006590_2.pdf.

MEXT. 2020b. *Current status of temporary school closure (in Japanese).* Accessed June 10, 2020. https://www.mext.go.jp/content/20200424-mxt_kouhou01-000004520_8.pdf.

MEXT. 2020c. *Status of schools' recommencement (in Japanese).* Accessed June 10, 2020. https://www.mext.go.jp/content/20200603-mxt_kouhou01-000004520_4.pdf.

MEXT. 2020d. *Actual condition of public schools under the condition of COVID-19 (in Japanese).* Accessed June 10, 2020. https://www.mext.go.jp/content/20200421-mxt_kouhou01-000006590_1.pdf.

MEXT. 2020e. *ICT use at home during the school closure (in Japanese).* Accessed June 10, 2020. https://www.mext.go.jp/content/20200424-mxt_jogai02-000003278_515.pdf.

MEXT. 2020f. *Extra budget in 2020 (in Japanese).* Accessed June 10, 2020. https://www.mext.go.jp/content/20200408-mxt_jogai02-000003278_412.pdf.

MEXT 2020g. *Emergent economic stimulus package (in Japanese).* Accessed June 10, 2020. https://www.mext.go.jp/content/20200407-mxt_kouhou02-000004520-3.pdf.

MEXT. 2020h. *General measures packages to guarantee students' learning (in Japanese).* Accessed June 10, 2020. https://www.mext.go.jp/content/20200605_mxt_kouhou02_000007000-1.pdf.

MEXT. 2020i. *Current status of teaching in public schools under the condition of COVID-19 (in Japanese).* Accessed June 10, 2020.

https://www.mext.go.jp/content/20200421-mxt_kouhou01-000004520_4.pdf.

MEXT. 2019. *Basic survey on schools (in Japanese).* Accessed June 10, 2020. https://www.mext.go.jp/content/20191220-mxt_chousa01-000003400_1.pdf.

MEXT. online1. *Website for supporting children's study (in Japanese).* Accessed June 10, 2020. https://www.mext.go.jp/a_menu/ikusei/gakusyushien/index_00001.htm

MEXT. online2. *GIGA school initiative (in Japanese).* Accessed June 10, 2020. https://www.mext.go.jp/a_menu/other/index_00001.htm.

MEXT. online3. *Informatization of education (in Japanese).* Accessed June 10, 2020. https://www.mext.go.jp/a_menu/shotou/zyouhou/index.htm.

MEXT. online4. *Reform on teachers' way of working (in Japanese).* Accessed June 10, 2020. https://www.mext.go.jp/a_menu/shotou/hatarakikata/index.htm.

NIER. 2019. *Summary of OECD PISA 2018 (in Japanese).* Accessed June 10, 2020. https://www.nier.go.jp/kokusai/pisa/pdf/2018/01_point.pdf.

NIER. 2018a. *Pupils' ICT use survey on OECD Programme for International Student Assessment (in Japanese).* Accessed June 10, 2020. https://www.nier.go.jp/kokusai/pisa/pdf/2018/06_supple.pdf.

NIER. 2018b. *The Work Environment of Teachers in Japan.* Accessed June 10, 2020. https://www.nier.go.jp/English/educationjapan/pdf/20180816WEJT.pdf

NIKKEI Asian Review. 2020. *Japan weighs change to its traditional April start of school year: PM Abe considering 'wide range of options' as coronavirus shutdown continues.* Accessed June 10, 2020. https://asia.nikkei.com/Business/Education/Japan-weighs-change-to-its-traditional-April-start-of-school-year.

OECD. 2020. *Learning remotely when schools close: How well are students and schools prepared? Insights from PISA.* Accessed June 10, 2020. https://read.oecd-ilibrary.org/view/?ref=127_127063-iiwm328658&title=Learning-remotely-when-schools-close.

OECD. 2012. *Students, Computers and Learning: Making the Connection Country note Japan.* Accessed June 10, 2020. https://www.oecd.org/pisa/keyfindings/PISA-2012-students-computers-japan.pdf.

OHCHR. 2020. *The Committee on the Rights of the Child warns of the grave physical, emotional and psychological effect of the COVID-19 pandemic on children and calls on States to protect the rights of children.* Accessed June 10, 2020. https://tbinternet.ohchr.org/Treaties/CRC/Shared20Documents/1_Global/INT_CRC_STA_9095_E.pdf.

Papamamastartup. 2020. *Current status of ICT adoption of schools in Tokyo (in Japanese).* Accessed June 10, 2020. https://papamamastartup.com/columns/344/.

Pattersen, Larry. 1993. *"Japan's 'Cram Schools." The Challenge of Higher Standards* 50(5):56-58. Accessed June 10, 2020. http://www.ascd.org/publications/educational-leadership/feb93/vol50/num05/Japan's-%E2%80%9CCram-Schools%E2%80%9D.aspx.

ReseMom. 2020. *A free-of-charge online juku will open 11th of May (in Japanese)*. Accessed June 10, 2020. https://resemom.jp/article/2020/04/30/56069.html.

ReseMom Biz. 2020. *Toshin opens two online courses for free of charge (in Japanese)* Accessed June 10, 2020. https://resemom.jp/article/2020/04/09/55745.html.

Save the Children Japan. 2020. *Report of urgent inquiry (in Japanese)* Accessed June 10, 2020. https://www.savechildren.or.jp/jpnem/jpn/pdf/kodomonokoe202005_report.pdf.

Sendai city. Online. *Scientific study on motivation in learning (in Japanese)* Accessed June 10, 2020. https://www.city.sendai.jp/manabi/kurashi/manabu/kyoiku/inkai/kanren/kyoiku/project.html.

Studyplus. 2018. *90% of high school students have studies using smartphone (in Japanese)* Accessed June 10, 2020. https://info.studyplus.co.jp/2018/07/17/986.

Sundai. online. Accessed June 10, 2020. https://www2.sundai.ac.jp/yobi/sv/index.html.

The Japan Times. 2020. *Private English tests for Japan university entrance exams delayed after minister's gaffe.* Accessed June 10, 2020.

https://www.japantimes.co.jp/news/2019/11/01/national/private-english-tests-for-university-exams-delayed-gaffe/.

Thoshin. online. Accessed June 10, 2020. https://www.toshin.com/index.php.

UNICEF. 2012. *Measuring child poverty: New league tables of child poverty in the world's rich countries.* UNICEF Innocenti Research Centre, Report Card 10, Accessed June 10, 2020. https://www.unicef-irc.org/publications/pdf/rc10_eng.pdf.

Voluntary group of Musashino city. Online. Accessed June 10, 2020. https://www.facebook.com/109514507408591/posts/120530186307023/.

Washington post. 2020. *1.5 billion children around globe affected by school closure. What countries are doing to keep kids learning during pandemic.* Accessed June 10, 2020. https://www.washingtonpost.com/education/2020/03/26/nearly-14-billion-children-around-globe-are-out-school-heres-what-countries-are-doing-keep-kids-learning-during-pandemic/

BIOGRAPHICAL SKETCH

Yutaro Ohashi

Affiliation: Nippon Institute of Technology

Education: PhD Keio University, Graduate School of Media and Governance, Fujisawa, Japan, 2018.

Research and Professional Experience: He has been conducting research on service learning and project-based learning in computer science education, game-based learning environment design, and ICT use in informal learning setting. His research projects received several awards including Good Design Award, Kids Design Award, and an educational award hosted by the Ministry of Education, Culture, Sports, Science and Technology, Japan.

Professional Appointments: Associate professor of Department of Information Technology and Media Design in Nippon Institute of Technology, Japan.

Honors:

1. 2020 8th International Conference on Information and Education Technology (ICIET 2020), Best Presentation Award, "Development of a Programming Course for Senior Citizens Taught by Senior Citizens," March 2020
2. Outstanding Reviewer's Award, IEEE International Conference on Teaching, Assessment and Learning for Engineering (TALE) 2018, December 2018
3. Emerging Scholar Award, Aging & Society: Eighth Interdisciplinary Conference, "Gameplay of an Older Adult with Mild Cognitive Impairment," September 2018

Publications from the Last 3 Years:

1. Ohashi, Y., and Yamachi, H. (2020) "Educational Effects of a Computer Programming Course for Teachers in Special Needs Education School and the Considerations Needed for Program Effectiveness (in Japanese)," *IPSJ Transactions on Computers and Education,* to appear.
2. Ohashi, Y., et al. (2020) "The effect of a Computer Programming Course on Elementary School Teachers' Awareness of Programming Education (in Japanese)," *Journal of Japanese Society for Engineering Education*, to appear.
3. Ohashi, Y., et al. (2020) "Development of a Programming Course for Senior Citizens Taught by Senior Citizens" *Proc. of the 8th*

International Conference on Information and Education Technology (ICIET 2020), 18-23.

4. Ohashi, Y., et al. (2019) "Knowledge Sharing and Teaching Ability Improvement of Teaching Assistants and Student Assistants in a First-Year Computer Programming Course (in Japanese)," *Journal Japanese Society for Engineering Education,* 67(1) 54-59.
5. Ohashi, Y., et al. (2019) "Comparison of Educational Video Production Methods for Students Studying Computer Programming," *Proc. of the 7th International Conference on Information and Education Technology (ICIET 2019),* 105-110.
6. Ohashi, Y., et al. (2018) "Readiness of Japanese Elementary School Teachers to Begin Computer-Programming Education," *Proc. of 2018 IEEE International Conference on Teaching, Assessment, and Learning for Engineering (TALE).*

In: Computers in Education
Editor: Ganelon Metivier
ISBN: 978-1-53618-612-3

Chapter 2

CONNECTING TECHNOLOGY IMMUNE–TECHNOLOGY ENABLED MATHEMATICS PEDAGOGY TO THE THEORY OF INSTRUMENTAL GENESIS

Sergei Abramovich*
State University of New York at Potsdam, NY, US

ABSTRACT

This chapter aims to demonstrate connections that exist between the notion of technology immune – technology enabled (TITE) mathematics problem-solving pedagogy and the theory of instrumental genesis. This theory has been used by educational researchers, including those in mathematics education, to study how the modern-day pedagogical appropriation of an artifact as a material object and the adaptation of this object to become an instrument as a psychological concept, in support of carrying out a particular task, take shape. TITE pedagogy gives credence to the idea that a mathematical problem cannot be outsourced entirely to a digital tool capable of diverse numeric and symbolic computations as

* Corresponding Author's E-mail: abramovs@potsdam.edu.

well as graphic constructions; yet the role of this tool plays fairly significant role in dealing with the problem. This chapter describes how the joint use of four digital instruments makes it possible to consider a mathematical task as an evolving exploration because each such tool, when, depending on purpose and function, used as either discrete or interdependent, allows for a specific extension of the task. The chapter includes illustrations, drawn from algebra and number theory, that are relevant to the secondary and tertiary levels of mathematics education. Teacher candidates' solicited comments about the use of technology are shared as appropriate.

Keywords: mathematics, technology, TITE pedagogy, instrumental genesis, teacher education

1. INTRODUCTION

The goal of this chapter is to show how the notion of technology immune – technology enabled (TITE) mathematics problem-solving pedagogy (Abramovich, 2014) can be connected to the theory of instrumental genesis (Rabardel, 1995). This theory has been used by educational researchers (Béguin and Rabardel, 2000; Rabardel and Bourmaud, 2003; Lonchamp, 2012; Ritella and Hakkarainen, 2012; Cerratto Pargman, Nouri, and Milrad, 2018), including mathematics educators (Guin and Trouche, 2002; Hegedus and Moreno-Armella, 2010; Roorda, Vos, Drijvers, and Goedhart, 2016), to study how the modern-day pedagogical appropriation of an artifact as a material object and the adaptation of this object to become an instrument as a psychological concept, in support of carrying out a particular task, take shape. The instrumental genesis theory has its origin in the seminal ideas by Lev Vygotsky about mediating cognitive processes, learning included, by physical tools and psychological instruments. According to Vygotsky (1930)[1], "What makes the instrumental act particularly unique is the

[1] Throughout the chapter, this work by Vygotsky, published on-line as an English translation from (most likely) a Russian source, will be cited frequently with no page numbers included.

simultaneous presence of stimuli of both kinds, i.e., of object [e.g., a problem to solve] and tool [e.g., a problem-solving strategy necessary to solve the problem] at the same time, each of which plays a qualitatively and functionally distinct role. Thus, in the instrumental act a new middle term is inserted between the object [a problem] and the mental operation [an intent to solve the problem] directed at it: the psychological tool, which becomes the structural center or focus, i.e., the aspect that functionally determines all the processes that form the instrumental act."

In the context of computer use in mathematics education, a digital tool being inserted between a problem solver (a subject) and a problem (an object), acts bi-directionally. On the one hand, the tool is used as a cognitive amplifier in solving a problem, e.g., it frees a problem solver from required computations, both numeric and symbolic, and, thereby, it acts primarily towards solving the problem. On the other hand, the use of the tool and its adaptation may not be straightforward which means that the appropriation of the tool motivates and often gives birth to various specific intellectual efforts on the part of the problem solver in order to be adapted for solving the problem. In other words, the tool acts towards the cognitive development of the user, thereby effecting solution of the problem. In the words of Vygotsky (1930), "Mental processes ... are directed toward the solution of a problem posed by the object, and the tool dictates their coordination and course. They form a new whole – the instrumental act." In mathematics education, the use of digital tools can change the course of problem solving by prompting alternative solution strategies which are due to the ease of computations, richness of modeling data, and the abundance of on-line information. At the same time, digital tools as artifacts "have potentials that the user may or may not develop ... [becoming evident after] the developments will be tried out, validated or rejected and artifacts will take on functions that will be temporary or permanent, following the diversity of the situations and projects the users set for themselves" (Béguin and Rabardel, 2000, p. 186). Thus, the important role of a mathematics educator at any grade level is to act both as a partner in epistemic advancement and a 'more knowledgeable other' when an instrumental act guides the process of education.

A TITE problem-solving pedagogy, born in the era of sophisticated digital tools, can be seen as an extension of Type II vs Type I uses of technology framework (Maddux, 1984) with its emphasis on "new and *better* ways of teaching" (p. 38, italics in the original) rather than using computers primarily for drill and practice (Type I). This modern-day pedagogy gives credence to the idea that a mathematical problem may not be outsourced entirely to a digital tool capable of diverse numeric and symbolic computations as well as graphic constructions; yet the role of this tool plays fairly significant (if not crucial) role in dealing with the problem. Once again, as Vygotsky (1930) put it, "The inclusion of a tool in the behavioral process ... abolishes and makes unnecessary a number of natural processes, whose work is [now] done by the tool."

Within a TITE problem-solving context, mathematical reasoning and digital computation go hand in hand enabling the appropriate use of digital tools. At the same time, a teacher candidate shared with the author that "one downside to these tools, they offer the easy way out for students. Instead of putting in the effort and going through the steps to solve the problem, they can simply put in the numbers in these tools and have the answer given to them. Like all things, there are always pros and cons." This position properly describes the very genesis of the TITE idea and supports the author's didactical perspective that, in particular, by learning to solve a TITE problem, one develops skills of distinguishing between positive and negative affordances of high-level digital tools, skills that are conducive to conceptual applications of computers. That is, a problem to be solved, in the words of Vygotsky (1930), serves as "a means by means of which we direct and realize the psychological operations ... necessary for the solution of the problem." Mathematical problem solving in the context of TITE pedagogy may appropriate several computer applications (digital tools) in support of a single task. In many cases, using different digital tools – numeric, symbolic, graphic – in addition to the enhancement of problem solving, enables a student, under the guidance of a teacher, to reflect on computationally obtained results. In particular, such guided reflection can lead to the development of another important skill – posing a new mathematical problem which may even go beyond the boundaries of the original problem-solving context.

2. From Artifact to Instrument

Nowadays, computers are commonly used as technical devices and the symbolic language of mathematics serves as a psychological tool that mediates thinking as a high-level mental activity associated with the use of computers. Turning an artifact into an instrument may not be an easy undertaking. For example, an electronic spreadsheet designed originally for non-educational purposes, was later "retrofitted" (Kaput, 1992) by mathematics educators to be used as "an electronic blackboard and electronic chalk in a classroom" (Power, 2000). At the very basic level, a spreadsheet can play the role of a simple calculator thus making the difference between the artifact and the instrument almost indistinguishable. In that case, one can say that a spreadsheet acts without affecting intellectual development of the user. However, it should be noted that even the use of a simple calculator, as an instrumental act, does create a residual mental power as any unsophisticated user of a calculator, including a young student, inadvertently commits to memory at least some results of calculations and, as a result, is able to carry out similar calculations by engaging memory.

Perhaps such use of a calculator as an instrumental act is similar to what Verillon and Rabardel (1995) called "a simplified example of instrumental genesis: a baby learning to use a spoon … [a process through which] he acquires some knowledge about the behavior of liquids [e.g., milk] as opposed, say, to mashed potatoes" (p. 85). Yet, at a more advanced level, a concept-laden mathematical use of a spreadsheet requires specialized knowledge of how to turn an artifact into an instrument. In the author's experience, this kind of knowledge is essential for the design of spreadsheets capable of the variety of mathematical modeling techniques ranging from a visual comparison of fractions (Abramovich, Stanton, and Baer, 2002) to computational experiments of coin tossing and die rolling

(Abramovich and Nikitin, 2017). A dual role of spreadsheets in mathematics education was recognized by one of the author's students who claimed, "Spreadsheets allow students to learn how to do calculations quickly and accurately ... [and] also how to build analytical thinking skills". This claim is echoed in another student's admission, "I am not a gifted mathematician, but I learned that using technology is an excellent way to allow multiple means of expression in mathematics ... technology gives freedom that is needed to make those expressions possible. In other words, multiple means of engagement lead to multiple means of expression by the student in mathematics and is an enrichment of learning." This credence also points at the fact that TITE pedagogy enables "multiple means of expression in mathematics" through the harmony of argument and computation. The faculty of the modern-day instrumental act, as another student believes, "improves [one's] excitement, motivation, and self-discovery." It appears that the students' focus on freedom of engagement and self-discovery through the use of technology is consistent with a philosophical idea that emphasizing children's "liberty, the sole means, will lead to the maximum development of character, intelligence and sentiment" (Montessori, 1917, p. 6).

Similarly, *Wolfram Alpha* – a computational knowledge engine available free on-line (as well as by relatively inexpensive subscription that gives access to its *Wolfram Alpha Pro* version) and capable of computations on a scale from simple numeric multiplication to sophisticated symbolic integration can be used both as an artifact and as an instrument for a variety of mathematical tasks. For example, as an artifact it can do same numeric calculations as a spreadsheet with similar residual mental power outcomes. The instrumental capability of its free (or paid) version can significantly complement a spreadsheet, yet an effective transition from artifact to instrument in the context of *Wolfram Alpha* requires one to possess both conceptual knowledge of mathematics and at least some level of mastery of the Wolfram Language.

After an artifact is turned into an instrument, the latter becomes inserted between the subject (a user of digital technology) and the object (a task) and, as was already mentioned, can act bi-directionally; that is, affecting both the completion of the task and intellectual development of the user. By acting towards the completion of the task, an instrument evinces pragmatic mediation and by acting towards the user it supports epistemic mediation (Lonchamp, 2012). This duality of the role of an instrument in problem solving allows one to see the TITE concept through the lens of the theory of instrumental genesis. Indeed, whereas during a TE stage of activity an instrument extends its instrumental sophistication, during a TI stage of activity, including the transformation of an artifact into an instrument, the subject grows in his/her cognitive power.

Put another way, a TI part of problem solving may be construed as "*instrumentation*" – a process through which a subject (i.e., a user of a digital tool) develops intellectually (e.g., by selecting appropriate mathematical concepts to be used in computing applications); its TE part may be construed as "*instrumentalization*" – a process through which an artifact (i.e., a digital tool) broadens the realm of utilization and becomes an instrument. As Lonchamp (2012) put it, "In the instrumentation process, the subject develops, while in the instrumentalization process, the artifact evolves" (p. 216). Within a TITE activity, its TI part represents the subject's thinking about how to use software as an instrument which mediates problem solving – this can be seen as the process of instrumentation because the use of software (a high-tech artifact) shapes this thinking. By the same token, a TE part represents the case when software, after being transformed into an instrument, enables the process of instrumentalization due to which the resolution of a particular problem/situation can be computationally enhanced as a new application of software has been developed. A TITE classroom pedagogy, as a teacher candidate put it, helps students "become more familiar with technology which is becoming a thing of the future that we all rely on in some way or another. It can also help promote a clearer understanding of certain problems that they may not understand how to achieve on paper or on their own." In the words of another teacher candidate, "if a student understands a mathematical concept, using technology ... could provide further explanation or a new explanation entirely that the student and teacher did not talk about yet." In these comments one can see how the blend of instrumentalization and instrumentation makes TITE pedagogy congruent with an instrumental act.

It should be noted that just as TI mathematical and TE technological activities can differ in complexity on the spectrum from basic to advanced, one may distinguish between basic and advanced instrumental acts as a subject turns an artifact into an instrument. Such distinction, however, bears a relative meaning because what is a basic for one may be an advanced for another and vice versa. Notwithstanding, an ability to extend the application of a basic instrumental act to new contexts can turn it into an advanced blend of instrumentation and instrumentalization. By the same token, the repeated use of an advanced instrumental act in multiple contexts transforms the advanced into the basic yet at a higher cognitive level (Abramovich, Nikitina, Romanenko, 2010).

3. Using Multiple Instruments as Double Stimulation

A TITE mathematical problem solving may include the use of multiple artifact-turned-instrument digital devices in support of a single task. In the case when the devices are complementary, such use of technology may be considered through the lens of double stimulation in support of a subject who is assigned a specific task or extends the assignment in a computational discovery fashion. The method of double stimulation is based on the idea of "using two sets of stimuli, one the primary set that has to be mastered and the other an auxiliary set that can serve as an instrument for mastering the primary set" (Luria, 2006, p. 47). A classic example of double stimulation is a piece of paper put on the floor as a second stimulus (a psychological instrument) enabling a Parkinson's patient to master making a step as the first stimulus (Vygotsky, 1962).

In the digital era, a pedagogy of exploring traditional problems of mathematics (including algebraic and number theory tasks relevant for secondary or tertiary curriculum) can be looked at as the use of the method of double stimulation. For instance, in proving the (mathematically well known) identity

$$1^3 + 2^3 + 3^3 + ... + n^3 = (1 + 2 + 3 + ... + n)^2 \qquad (1)$$

– the first stimulus – a subject can first extend (basic instrumentalization) the spreadsheet (Figure 1) filled with consecutive natural numbers (column A) and their cubes (column C) to numerically model partial sums of the natural numbers (column B) and their cubes (column D) and, finally, the squares of the former sums (column E). Comparing numbers in columns D and E confirms numerically identity (1) for the first five values of *n*.

	A	B	C	D	E
1	n	1+2+...+n	n^3	1^3+2^3+...+n^3	(1+2+...+n)^2
2	1	1	1	1	1
3	2	3	8	9	9
4	3	6	27	36	36
5	4	10	64	100	100
6	5	15	125	225	225
7	6	21	216	441	441
8	7	28	343	784	784
9	8	36	512	1296	1296
10	9	45	729	2025	2025
11	10	55	1000	3025	3025

Figure 1. Basic instrumentation using a spreadsheet.

Then, using *Wolfram Alpha*, the subject can enter in its input box the commands "sum i, i = 1 to n" and "sum i^3, i = 1 to n" to find, respectively, that

$$1 + 2 + 3 + ... + n = n(n+1)/2 \text{ and}$$

$$1^3 + 2^3 + 3^3 + ... + n^3 = n^2(n+1)^2/4\,. \qquad (2)$$

This on-line "discovery" of formulas (2) confirms symbolically that identity (1) is true. Mastering proof (the first set of stimuli) was due to the second set of stimuli that may be referred to as an integrated spreadsheet (Abramovich, 2016) for it consists of two rather distinct devices having complementary computational capability – numeric and symbolic. One can see how integrating two commonly available digital tools can be used in proving an algebraic identity through a combination of numerical verification and on-line "discovery," thus indicating that, indeed, "double stimulation is not a mechanical process; the prevailing instruments and procedures have to be creatively adapted for solving the problems encountered" (Ritella and Hakkarainen, 2012, p. 245). Also, using two digital tools (that is, working in a TE fashion or enabling instrumentalization) not only provides support for solving a problem (the first stimulus) but it can motivate one's deep thinking (belonging to the second set of stimuli working epistemically in a TI fashion or enabling instrumentation) about computationally obtained results.

4. An Interplay of TI and TE Activities

A TI part of a TITE activity can be at least of two types. The first type is when one uses mathematical concepts as tools in computing applications with the goal to turn an artifact into an instrument. One such example is the use of recursive definitions ($x_n = x_{n-1} + 1, x_1 = 1$ and $s_n = s_{n-1} + x_n, s_1 = 1$) of natural numbers x_n and their partial sums s_n, respectively, in programming the spreadsheet of Figure 2. The second type of a TI part of a TITE activity, depending on an instrument used, may include the need to analyze and make sense of numeric, symbolic, graphic, or even verbal information. For example, one can note (Figure 1) that just as every number in column C is divisible by the corresponding number in column A, many numbers in column B (but not all) are divisible by three. This, essentially TI, observation can prompt a simple TE follow-up activity: by using the MOD(a, b) function which yields the remainder of a divided by *b*, a spreadsheet can generate the sequence of remainders when the partial sums of consecutive natural numbers are divided by three (instrumentalization). As shown in the spreadsheet of Figure 2, this sequence conforms to the following pattern: 1, 0, 0, 1, 0, 0, 1, 0, 0, 1, 0, 0, ... As a result, one can be motivated to explore this phenomenon in a TI fashion.

	A	B	C
1	n	1+2+...+n	3
2	1	1	1
3	2	3	0
4	3	6	0
5	4	10	1
6	5	15	0
7	6	21	0
8	7	28	1
9	8	36	0
10	9	45	0
11	10	55	1
12	11	66	0
13	12	78	0

Figure 2. Multiples of three among triangular numbers.

In the words of Vygotsky (1930), "The mastery of a psychological tool and, through it, of one's own natural mental function, always lifts the given function to a higher level, enhances and broadens its activity, recreates its structure and mechanism." Indeed, one can enter the above sequence in the input box of the Online Encyclopedia of Integer Sequences (OEIS®, https://oeis.org), a rich source of mathematical knowledge, to find the sequence under the number A079978 and being referred to, among other concepts, as the characteristic function of multiples of three along with the decimal expansion of 1/999 (which can be generated by *Wolfram Alpha* as one enters this fraction in the input box of the program). Also, *Wolfram Alpha* describes this sequence in the form $x_n = 2n^2 + 2n \mod 3$, something that can be verified by using a spreadsheet (the basic instrumentation through the use of the formula $=\mathrm{mod}(2n^2+2n,3)$ with the natural numbers n located in a separate column). Such a variety of concepts and interpretations that different tools, both artifacts and instruments, make available raises an issue of how a subject can manage the abundance of information with an easy access (Conole and Dyke, 2004). That is, exploring the partial sums of consecutive natural numbers can provide either artifact-based or instrument-based information that may not be originally expected to be obtained (or, in the words of a teacher candidate already cited above, "the student and teacher did not talk about yet"), and, thereby, cannot be easily understood, let alone meaningfully interpreted, by a subject.

Such a TE activity can motivate a follow up explanation of the "division by three" outcome in a TI fashion. In particular, one has to explain why among any three consecutive partial sums of consecutive natural numbers (starting from the number 1) two sums are divisible by three and one sum when divided by three yields remainder 1. To this end, first note that the sum of any three consecutive natural numbers is divisible by three. Indeed, such sum has the form $n+(n+1)+(n+2)=3n+3=3(n+1)$; in other words, the sum is three times as big as its second term. Also, among the first three partial sums of consecutive natural numbers – 1, 1 + 2, and 1 + 2 + 3 – the second and the third sums are divisible by three. Then, all such triples of partial sums of consecutive natural numbers starting from the number 1 will be generated by 1, 1 + 2 (= 3), and 1 + 2 + 3 (= 6), respectively, as follows:

$$1+\underbrace{(2+3+4)}_{\textit{divisible by 3}}+\underbrace{(5+6+7)}_{\textit{divisible by 3}}+\ldots+\underbrace{(3n-1)+3n+(3n+1)}_{\textit{divisible by 3}}+\ldots=\{1,10,28,\ldots\};$$

$$\underbrace{1+2}_{\textit{divisible by 3}}+\underbrace{(3+4+5)}_{\textit{divisible by 3}}+\underbrace{(6+7+8)}_{\textit{divisible by 3}}+\ldots+\underbrace{3n+(3n+1)+(3n+2)}_{\textit{divisible by 3}}+\ldots=\{3,15,36,\ldots\};$$

and

$$\underbrace{1+2+3}_{divisible\ by\ 3}+\underbrace{(4+5+6)}_{divisible\ by\ 3}+\underbrace{(7+8+9)}_{divisible\ by\ 3}+...+\underbrace{(3n+1)+(3n+2)+(3n+3)}_{divisible\ by\ 3}+...=\{6,21,45,...\}$$

.

One can see that starting from the number 1, every fourth partial sum when divided by three yields the remainder 1, and all other partial sums are divisible by 3. This example demonstrates how TE and TI parts of an instrumental act go hand in hand, support each other, and serve as a means for motivating new TITE activities. The next section provides an example of how multiple digital tools can be used in support of such motivation.

5. TITE Problem Posing as an Instrumental Act

A solved problem can be used as a stimulus for posing a new problem. That is, whereas a psychological instrument does not change the original stimulus (an object in the form of a problem to be solved), an instrumental act can motivate the subject's reflection on the problem in the form of a "what if?" question directed towards the solved problem. In that case, the original stimulus, while not being changed, plays the role of a psychological tool of the instrumental act directed towards the subject. As an illustration, consider the sequence t_n of triangular numbers

1, 3, 6, 10, 15, 21, 28, 36, 45, 55, 66, 78, 91, 105, 120, 136, 153, ... (3)

A subsequence $t_{n,k}$ of triangular numbers t_n developed through k successive eliminations of every other triangular number from the resulting subsequence which survives each elimination will be referred to as the triangular number sieve of order k. That is, the sequence of triangular numbers t_n is the triangular number sieve of order zero; the subsequence 1, 6, 15, 28, 45, 66, 91, 120, 153, ... , is the triangular number sieve of order one; the subsequence 1, 15, 45, 91, 153, ... , is the triangular number sieve of order two; the subsequence 1, 45, 153, ... , is the triangular number sieve of order three, and so on. As shown in (Abramovich, 2019a, p. 187), one can prove using the method of mathematical induction by the variable k (a TI part of new activities) that

$$t_{n,k} = [2^k(n-1)+1][2^{k-1}(n-1)+1]. \tag{4}$$

For example, when $n = 2$ and $k = 4$ we have $t_{2,4} = (8+1)(16+1) = 153$ – the second term of the triangular number sieve of order four. Alternatively, the triangular number sieve of order k can be developed if one starts with the number 1 and eliminates the next $2^k - 1$ (consecutive) triangular numbers to get the second term, then eliminates the next $2^k - 1$ (consecutive) triangular numbers to get the third term, and so on. Indeed, one can check with the sequence of triangular numbers (3) to see that between the numbers 1 and 45 there are $2^3 - 1 = 7$ triangular numbers; likewise, seven triangular numbers are located between 45 and 153. This observation is not only a recipe for a hands-on elimination, it may motivate a new spreadsheet-based instrumentation as an alternative to formula (4). Towards this end, note that the ranks of the triangular numbers 1, 45, 153, 325, 351, 561, ... , are, respectively, 1, 9, 17, 25, 33, ..., - consecutive terms of the arithmetic sequence with the first term 1 and difference 8. The terms of this sequence have the form $8n - 7$, $n = 1, 2, 3, ...$ Consequently, using the first formula from (2), the triangular numbers 1, 45, 153, 325, 351, 561,..., can be written as $\frac{(8n-7)(8n-6)}{2} = (8n-7)(4n-3)$. One can check to see that the resulting product is exactly $t_{n,3}$ defined through formula (4). The corresponding spreadsheet-based TE extension (or instrumentalization) of this TI activity (or instrumentation) is shown in Figure 3. (The emphasis on the difference 300 will be explained later). That is,

$$t_{n,3} = (8n-7)(4n-3). \tag{5}$$

D	E	F	G	H
3	Elimination		Formula (4)	Difference
1	1		1	
9	45		45	44
17	153		153	108
25	325		325	172
33	561		561	236
41	861		861	300
49	1225		1225	364
57	1653		1653	428

Figure 3. Two ways of modeling the triangular number sieve of order three.

Seeing the numbers 8, 7, 4, 3 as, $2^3, 2^3-1, 2^{3-1}, 2^{3-1}-1$, respectively, allows one to generalize from (5) to get $t_{n,k} = (2^k n - 2^k + 1)(2^{k-1} n - 2^{k-1} + 1) = [2^k(n-1)+1][2^{k-1}(n-1)+1]$, exactly the form of the triangular number sieve of order *k* provided by formula (4). Alternatively, one can plug *k* = 3 in formula (4) to get formula (5). Such uncomplicated TI activities demonstrate that there is always a room for mathematical reasoning through which a formula can be used as a stimulus for verifying another formula and vice versa.

Input interpretation:

{1, 45, 153, 325, 561, 861, ...}

Possible sequence identification:

Closed form

$a_n = 32n^2 - 52n + 21$ (for all terms given)

Continuation

1, 45, 153, 325, 561, 861, 1225, 1653, 2145, 2701, 3321, 4005, 4753, 5565, 6441, ...

Figure 4. Confirming a TI-based finding through a TE-based query.

Returning to a TE agency of learning mathematics, it is always interesting to see if a sequence in question, in our case, 1, 45, 153, 325, 351, 561, ..., is included into the OEIS®. Whereas this sequence is not included into the OEIS®, its representation through the expanded form of the right-hand side of formula (5) can be confirmed by *Wolfram Alpha* (Figure 4).

One can also note that differences between two consecutive terms of the last sequence form the sequence 44, 108, 172, 236, 300, ... In particular, the number 300 is the difference between two consecutive terms of the sequence $t_{n,k}$ when $k = 3$ and $n = 5$. This enables one to pose the following

Problem. *It is known that the difference between two consecutive terms,* $t_{n+1,k}$ and $t_{n,k}$, *of a triangular number sieve of order k is equal to 300. Find k and n.*

In order to solve this problem, multiple artifacts can be used: the *Wolfram Alpha* as a symbolic manipulator along with the *Graphing Calculator* (Avitzur, 2011) and the *Geometer Sketchpad* (Jackiw, 1991, 2009) as two graphing tools. It is interesting to note that *Wolfram Alpha Pro* version provides users with 25 steps used in simplifying the difference (Figure 5, left) to the final form (Figure 5, right). Such use of *Wolfram Alpha Pro* in revealing a large number of steps needed to carry out a specific algebraic operation is an "instrumental act [in which] we see activity towards oneself, and not towards the object" (Vygotsky, 1930). Indeed, only the final form of the simplified difference is required for the purpose of using a graphing (or any other relevant digital) tool in solving the problem. At the same time, the recognition of the computational power of *Wolfram Alpha* which, in the words of Vygotsky (1930), "enhances and immensely extends the possibilities of behavior by making the results of the work of geniuses available to everyone," motivates the subject to continue using this instrument in the true spirit of the method of double stimulation as "an auxiliary set [of stimuli] that can serve as an instrument for mastering the primary set" (Luria, 2006, p. 47).

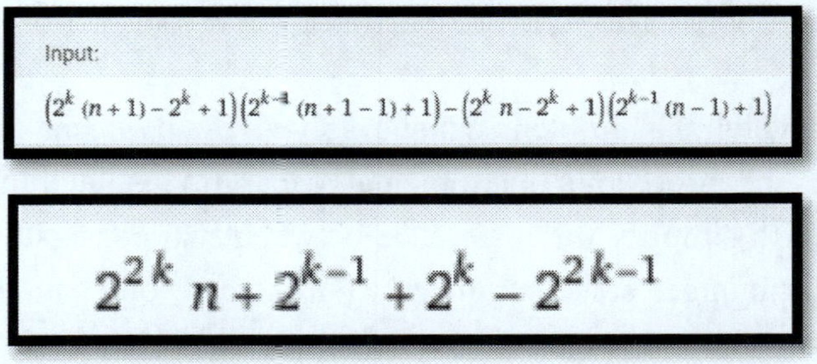

Figure 5. Using *Wolfram Alpha* as a symbolic manipulator.

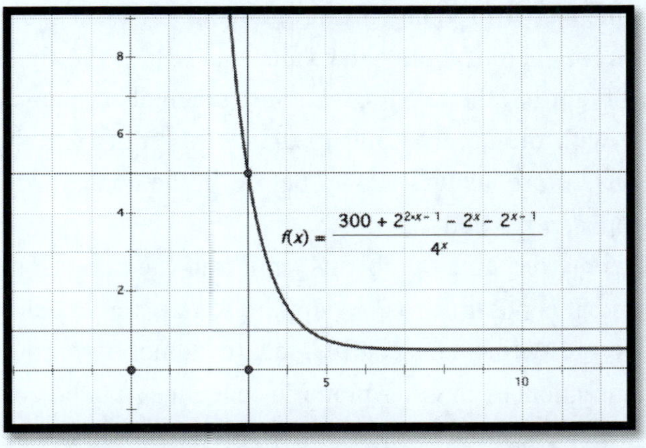

Figure 6. Graphing a function with the *Geometer's Sketchpad*.

The primary set of stimuli is the problem posed in the context of reflecting on numeric data generated by a spreadsheet. The problem can be solved graphically. To this end, one has to solve the relation $2^{2k}n+2^{k-1}+2^k-2^{2k-1}=300$ over n and k. There are two types of graphing software available: a function grapher and a relation grapher. An example of the former tool is the *Geometer's Sketchpad* the use of which requires representing n as a function of k. An example of the latter tool is the *Graphing Calculator* the use of which does not require such functional representation. The uses of both tools are shown, respectively, in Figure 6 and Figure 7. In the latter case, once a graph is constructed, one has to locate a point with whole number coordinates on the corresponding graph. In the former case, such point can be visually located and confirmed by graphing it. In both cases, one demonstrates the use of instrumentalization skills.

Alternatively, the problem can be solved by *Wolfram Alpha* using, once again, the program's instrumental capability, something that was already used to simplify the difference between two consecutive terms of the triangular number sieve of order *k*. To this end, one can enter into its input box the expression "Table[n2^(2k)+2^(k-1)+2^k-2^(2k-1), {n,8},{k,8}] in which, using *Wolfram* programming code as the act of instrumentation, the second and the third components of the command Table are aimed at instructing the program to create a table of eight *n* values, [1, 8], for each of the eight *k* values, [1, 8], of the first component. As shown in Figure 8, the result of this instrumental act is a square matrix of size eight with the number 300 located in the third *n*-column and the fifth *k*-row. Therefore, as was shown before in the context of plotting and exploring graphs, $n = 3$ and $k = 5$.

Using this matrix, many problems similar to the one just solved can be posed. For one, it is possible to consider the square number sieve of order *k* with $k = 0$ representing consecutive square numbers starting from one. Likewise, subsequences of other numeric sequences can be considered and explored in a TITE fashion using a combination of computer programs. For example, when eliminating every other number from a sequence, one eliminates every number the rank of which is a multiple of two. Another type of sieve can stem from eliminating every number the rank of which is a multiple of three (or four, five, and so on). Each elimination may begin within a spreadsheet (capable of recognizing ranks via the mod function discussed above) resulting in a sequence to be explored, as a new object, using several tools. The presence of a variety of objects and, most importantly, tools used to stimulate TITE mathematical behavior of a subject toward an object is the crux of the instrumental method as "any tool is without fail a stimulus: if it were not a stimulus, i.e., did not have the capacity to influence behavior, it could not be a tool" (Vygotsky, 1930).

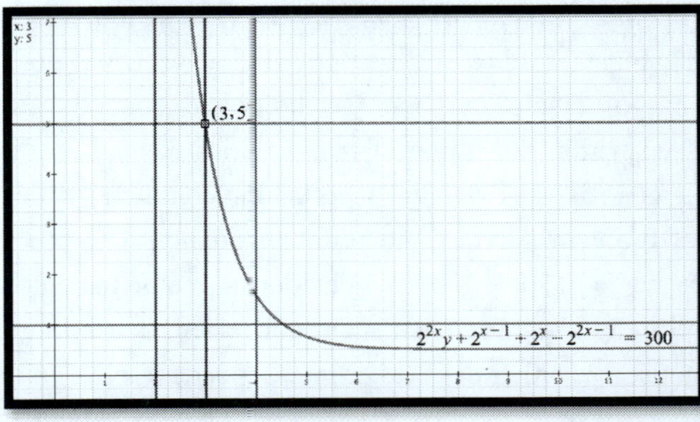

Figure 7. Graphing a relation with the *Graphing Calculator*.

Input:

Table$\left[n \times 2^{2k} + 2^{k-1} + 2^{k} - 2^{2k-1}, \{n, 8\}, \{k, 8\}\right]$

Result:

5	14	44	152	560	2144	8384	33 152
9	30	108	408	1584	6240	24 768	98 688
13	46	172	664	2608	10 336	41 152	164 224
17	62	236	920	3632	14 432	57 536	229 760
21	78	300	1176	4656	18 528	73 920	295 296
25	94	364	1432	5680	22 624	90 304	360 832
29	110	428	1588	6704	26 720	106 688	426 368
33	126	492	1944	7728	30 816	123 072	491 904

Figure 8. A matrix form of the difference generated by *Wolfram Alpha*.

CONCLUSION

This chapter's goal was to demonstrate connections between the theory of instrumental genesis and technology immune – technology enabled (TITE) mathematics problem-solving pedagogy. Several explorations with triangular numbers supported by multiple computer tools were used to illustrate those connections. Whereas the ideas of TITE pedagogy were developed in the context of mathematics education, the theory of instrumental genesis studies the uses of digital technologies across the wide spectrum of disciplines and psychological contexts. Nonetheless, when discussed within the frame of mathematics education, the theory of instrumental genesis has many aspects in common with the TITE mathematical problem solving and problem posing. The use of multiple digital tools made it possible to consider a mathematical task as an evolving exploration because each such tool, when, depending on purpose and function, used as either discrete or interdependent, allows for a specific extension of the task. This also made it possible to extend three major orientations of an instrument-mediated activity proposed by Rabardel and Bourmaud (2003) – toward the object (e.g., a problem to be solved), toward oneself (e.g., a user of a digital tool), and toward other subjects (e.g., students) – to include a specific for mathematics education orientation toward other objects construed as new problems posed by the subject through the process of epistemic mediation as new instrumentation ideas develop.

An interaction among four instruments – a spreadsheet, the *Geometer's Sketchpad*, the *Graphing Calculator* and *Wolfram Alpha* – was illustrated through exploring the so-called triangular number sieve of order three. The joint use of these digital tools enhanced credibility of instrument-mediated activities and underscored the importance of complementary nature of the digital tools involved. The orientation toward a new object is a natural characteristic of such instrumentally-diverse learning environments because problem solving and problem posing are closely related mathematical activities. Figure 9 shows the use of a spreadsheet as the first artifact-turned-instrument inserted between the subject (a problem solver) and the object (a problem to be solved). Orienting the spreadsheet towards the subject creates conditions conducive for the latter to pose a new problem which then becomes a new object. Three other instruments then become inserted between the subject and the new object and, by being both unique and complementary, they can act towards the subject in support of solving a new problem. First, *Wolfram Alpha* simplifies the difference between two consecutive terms of the general sieve, then the simplified expression becomes a two-variable equation to be solved graphically, and finally, the solution discovered on two (independently constructed) graphs is verified by locating it within a matrix provided by *Wolfram Alpha* through an advanced instrumentation. In that way, *Wolfram Alpha* as a psychological tool played a dual role in the process of TITE problem solving as an instrumental act. First, it epistemically mediated mathematical behavior of the subject by taking on complex algebraic simplification. Second, it pragmatically mediated this behavior by creating a conceptually intricate numerical milieu for verifying the correctness of solution already obtained by two structurally different tools. As noted by one of the leading mathematics educators of the second part of the 20th century, "It is independency of new experiments that enhances credibility" (Freudenthal, 1978, p. 193).

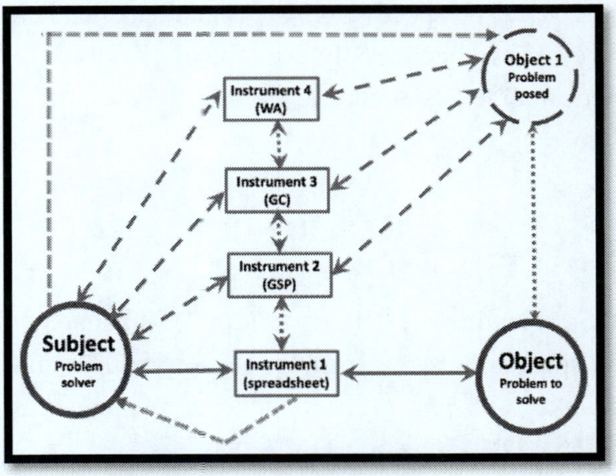

Figure 9. TITE problem solving and posing with multiple instruments.

Finally, the chapter demonstrated how the difference between basic and advanced instrumentations can be discussed in terms of the difference between artifacts. For example, whereas the construction of a two-variable equation in the context of the *Graphing Calculator* requires a basic instrumentation as the tool is capable of graphing such relations (e.g., $F(x, y) = 0$) without transforming them into a functional relation of the form $y = f(x)$, graphing in the context of the *Geometer's Sketchpad* requires more than a basic instrumentation for the latter tool can only graph functions. In the case of a non-linear relation, the transition from such a relation to its functional form often requires an advanced instrumentation. Furthermore, the level of instrumentation, in many respects, depends on a subject as well: what seems to be an advanced for one may be a basic for the other. It that sense, the orientation toward other subjects as proposed by Rabardel and Bourmaud (2003) and discussed elsewhere (Abramovich, 2019b) can be used as an instrument of professional development of teacher candidates within a teacher preparation program and of schoolteachers within a school or a school district. The array of artifacts available and the scope of their applications in a mathematics teacher education classroom support the diversity of teaching methods incorporating the ideas of instrumental genesis and TITE pedagogy. In that way, the instrumental perspective on TITE mathematics curriculum opens a window to new uses of commonly available digital tools to the benefit of diverse learners at all levels of education.

REFERENCES

Abramovich, S., Stanton, M., & Baer, E. (2002). What are Billy's chances? Computer spreadsheet as a learning tool for younger children and their teachers alike. *Journal of computers in mathematics and science teaching*, *21*, 127-145.

Abramovich, S., Nikitina, G. V., & Romanenko, V. N. (2010). Spreadsheets and the development of skills in the STEM disciplines. *Spreadsheets in education*, *3*(3), Article 5.

Abramovich S. (2014). Revisiting mathematical problem solving and posing in the digital era: toward pedagogically sound uses of modern technology. *International journal of mathematical education in science and technology*, *45*, 1034-1052.

Abramovich S. (2016). *Exploring mathematics with integrated spreadsheets in teacher education*. Singapore: World Scientific.

Abramovich, S., & Nikitin, Ya. Yu. (2017). Teaching classic probability problems with modern digital tools. *Computers in the schools*, *34*, 318-336.

Abramovich, S. (2019a). *Integrating computers and problem posing in mathematics teacher education*. Singapore: World Scientific.

Abramovich, S. (2019b). Technology-immune/technology-enabled mathematical problem solving as instrumental genesis. *Open mathematical education notes*, *9*, 23-54.

Avitzur, R. (2011). *Graphing Calculator* [Computer software, Version 4.1]. Berkeley, CA: Pacific Tech.

Béguin, P., & Rabardel, P. (2000). Designing instrument-mediated activity. *Scandinavian journal of information systems*, *12*, 173-190.

Cerratto Pargman, T., Nouri, J., & Milrad, M. (2018). Taking an instrumental genesis lens: New insights into collaborative mobile learning. *British journal of educational technology*, *49*, 219-234.

Conole, G., & Dyke, M. (2004). What are the affordances of information and communication technologies? *ALT-J: Research in learning technology*, *12*, 113-124.

Freudenthal, H. (1978). *Weeding and sowing*. Dordrecht, The Netherlands: Kluwer Academic Publishers.

Guin, D., & Trouche, L. (2002). Mastering by the teacher of the instrumental genesis in CAS environments: Necessity of instrumental orchestrations. *Zentralblatt für didaktik der mathematik*, *34*, 204-211.

Hegedus, S. J., & Moreno-Armella, L. (2010). Accommodating the instrumental genesis framework within dynamic technological environments. *For the learning of mathematics*, *30*, 26-31.

Jackiw, N. (1991, 2009). *The Geometer's Sketchpad* [Computer programs, Version 1-5]. Emeryville, CA: Key Curriculum Press.

Kaput, J. J. (1992). Technology and mathematics education. In D. A. Grouws (Ed.), *Handbook of research on mathematics teaching and learning*, (pp. 515-556). New York, NY: Macmillan.

Lonchamp, J. (2012). An instrumental perspective on CSCL systems. *International journal of computer-supported collaborative learning*, *7*, 211-237.

Luria, A. R. (2006). *The making of mind: A personal account of Soviet psychology*. Cole M., & Cole, S. (Eds). Mahwah, NJ: Lawrence Erlbaum.

Maddux, C. D. (1984). Educational microcomputing: The need for research. *Computers in the schools*, *1*, 35-41.

Montessori, M. (1917). *Spontaneous activity in education*. New York, NY: Frederick A. Stokes Publishers.

Power, D. J.(2000). *DSSResources.COM*. (http://dssresources.com/history/sshistory.html).

Rabardel, P. (1995). *Les hommes et les technologies, une approche cognitive des instruments contemporains* [*Men and technologies, a cognitive approach to contemporary instruments*]. Paris: Armand Colin.

Rabardel, P., & Bourmaud, G. (2003). From computer to instrument system. *Interacting with computers*, *15*, 665-691.

Ritella, G., & Hakkarainen, K. (2012). Instrumental genesis in technology-mediated learning: From double stimulation to expansive knowledge practices. *Computer-supported collaborative learning*, *7*, 239-258.

Roorda, G., Vos, P., Drijvers, P., & Goedhart, M. (2016). Solving rate of change tasks with a graphing calculator: A case study on instrumental genesis. *Digital experiences in mathematics education, 2*, 228-252.

Verillon, P., & Rabardel, P. (1995). Cognition and artifacts: A contribution to the study of thought in relation to instrumented activity. *European journal of psychology of education*, *10*, 77-101.

Vygotsky, L. S. (1930). The instrumental method in psychology (talk given in 1930 at the Krupskaya Academy of Communist Education). *Lev Vygotsky Archive*. [On-line materials]. Available at: https://www.marxists.org/archive/vygotsky/works/1930/instrumental.htm.

Vygotsky, L. S. (1962). *Thought and language*. Cambridge, MA: MIT Press.

BIOGRAPHICAL SKETCH

Sergei Abramovich

Affiliation: State University of New York at Potsdam, USA

Education: PhD, Saint Petersburg State University, Russia

Research and Professional Experience: Sergei Abramovich is Professor in the School of Education and Professional Studies at State University of New York at Potsdam. His current scholarly interests include projects dealing with experimental mathematics for teachers, technology and problem posing (including mathematics curriculum design), hidden mathematics curriculum of teacher education, the relationship between algorithmic thinking and conceptual knowledge, and early technology-enhanced mathematics experiences with an engineering/science focus. He is the author/co-author/editor of nine books and more than 200 articles on the use of computers in mathematics education. His service to educational community includes membership on editorial boards of eight professional journals published in the United States and elsewhere.

Professional Appointments: Open Mathematical Education Notes – founding Editor in Chief; Advances in Educational Research and Evaluation – founding Editor in Chief.

Honors: The State University of New York Chancellor's Award for Excellence in Scholarship and Creative Activities (2008)

Publications from the Last 3 Years:

1. Abramovich, S. (2019). Advances in education: from the Egyptian papyrus roll to signature pedagogies of the digital era (Editorial). *Advances in Educational Research and Evaluation*, 1(1), 1-5.

2. Abramovich, S., and Leonov, G. A. (2019). *Revisiting Fibonacci numbers through a computational experiment.* New York, NY: Nova Science Publishers.
3. Abramovich, S. (2019). *Integrating computers and problem posing in mathematics teacher education*. Singapore: World Scientific.
4. Abramovich, S. (2019). Technology-immune/technology-enabled mathematical problem solving as instrumental genesis. *Open Mathematical Education Notes*, 9(1), 23-54.
5. Abramovich, S., Grinshpan, A. Z., and Milligan, D. L. (2019). Teaching mathematics through concept motivation and action learning. *Educational Research International,* volume 2019, Article ID 3745406, 13 pages, http://doi.org/10.1155/2019/3745406.
6. Connell, M. and Abramovich, S. (2018). Aunt Sarah and the Farm: A guided tour of a spreadsheet exploration. In *Proceedings of E-Learn: World Conference on E-Learning in Corporate, Government, Healthcare, and Higher Education* (pp. 1386-1393). Las Vegas, NV, United States: Association for the Advancement of Computing in Education (AACE).
7. Abramovich, S. (2018). Diversity in mathematics teacher preparation in the era of Common Core: From Egyptian papyrus roll to Gestalt psychology to digital computation. In R. V. Nata (Ed.), *Progress in Education*, vol. 54 (pp. 1-36). New York, NY: Nova Science Publishers.
8. Abramovich, S. (2018). From the teaching machine movement to instrumental perspective on technology-immune/technology-enabled mathematics curriculum. *Informatics and Education*, 6(295), 58-64.
9. Kuznetsov, N. V., Abramovich, S., Fradkov, A. L. and Chen, R. (2018). In Memoriam: Gennady Alekseevich Leonov. *International Journal of Bifurcation and Chaos*, 28(5), 5 pages.
10. Abramovich, S., Kuznetsov, N. V, and Neittaanmäki, P. (2018). Obituary: Gennady Alekseevich Leonov (1947-2018). *Open Mathematical Education Notes*, 8(1), 15-21.

11. Connell, M., Abramovich, S., and Sack, J. (2018). Teaching and learning mathematics in technology intensive classrooms. In J. L. Nath and I. Chen (Eds), *Technology in the Classroom: For Now and the Future* (pp. 85-107). Second revised edition. Dubuque, IA: Kendall Hunt Publishing Company.
12. Abramovich, S. (2018). Technology and the development of creativity in advanced school mathematics. In V. Freiman and J. Tassell (Eds). *Creativity and Technology in Mathematics Education* (pp. 371-398). Cham, Switzerland: Springer.
13. Abramovich, S., and Nikitin, Ya. Yu. (2017). Teaching classic probability problems with modern digital tools. *Computers in the Schools*, 34(4), 318-336.
14. Abramovich, S., and Nikitin, Ya. Yu. (2017). On the probability of co-primality of two randomly chosen natural (Who was the first to pose and solve this problem?). *Mathematics in Higher Education*, 15, 53-68. (In Russian).
15. Lazić, B., Abramovich, S., Mrda, M, and Romano, D. A. (2017). On the teaching and learning of fractions through a conceptual generalization approach. *IEJME–Mathematics Education*, 12(8), 749-767.
16. Abramovich, S., and Connell, M. L. (2017). Revisiting mathematical activities for secondary teachers through the lenses of modern digital tools. *Open Mathematical Education Notes*, 7(1), 9-28.
17. Connell, M. L., and Abramovich, S. (2017). Burning the candle: A Technology Immune Technology Enabled problem within an Action on Objects framework. In J. Dron & S. Mishra (Eds), *Proceedings of 2017 E-Learn: World Conference on E-Learning in Corporate, Government, Healthcare, and Higher Education* (pp. 1724-1730). Association for the Advancement of Computing in Education.
18. Connell, M. L., and Abramovich, S. (2017). Stamping Functions: A Technology Immune Technology Enabled Problem within an Action on Objects Framework. In L. Liu & D. Gibson (Eds),

Research Highlights in Technology and Teacher Education 2017 (pp. 55-61). Association for the Advancement of Computing in Education (AACE). Available on-line at https://www.learntechlib.org/p/180960/

19. Abramovich, S., and Connell, M. L. (2017). Problem solving in the digital age: New ideas for secondary mathematics teacher education. *Journal of Computers in Mathematics and Science Teaching*, 36(2), 105-116.
20. Connell, M. L., and Abramovich, S. (2017). A technology immune technology enabled problem within an action on objects framework: Stamping functions. *Journal of Computers in Mathematics and Science Teaching*, 36(2), 117-127.
21. Abramovich, S., and Connell, M. L. (2017). TITE problem solving: integrating computing and proving in secondary mathematics teacher education. In P. Resta & S. Smith (Eds.), *Proceedings of Society for Information Technology & Teacher Education International Conference 2017* (pp. 1321-1327). Chesapeake, VA: Association for the Advancement of Computing in Education.
22. Connell, M. L., and Abramovich, S. (2017). STEM teaching and learning via technology enhanced inquiry. In I. Levin and D. Tsybulsky (Eds.), *Digital Tools and Solutions for Inquiry-Based STEM Learning*, Section 1: Inquiry-Based Learning of STEM in Digital Era, chapter 9 (pp. 221-251). Hershey, PA: IGI Global.
23. Connell, M. L., and Abramovich, S. (2017). Stamping Functions: A Technology Immune Technology Enabled Problem within an Action on Objects Framework. In In P. Resta & S. Smith (Eds.), *Proceedings of Society for Information Technology & Teacher Education International Conference 2017* (pp. 1328-1334). Chesapeake, VA: Association for the Advancement of Computing in Education.
24. Abramovich, S. (2017). Progress in mathematical problem posing: From "the liberty of the child" to computational experiments. In R.

V. Nata (Ed.), *Progress in Education, vol. 43* (pp. 49-69). New York, NY: Nova Science Publishers.

25. Abramovich, S. (2017). *Diversifying Mathematics Teaching: Advanced Educational Content and Methods for Prospective Elementary Teachers*. Singapore: World Scientific.
26. Abramovich, S., and Nikitin, Ya. Yu. (2017). On the probability of co-primality of two randomly natural numbers chosen at random: From Euler identity to Haar measure on the ring of adeles. *Bernoulli News*, 24(1), 7-13.

In: Computers in Education
Editor: Ganelon Metivier
ISBN: 978-1-53618-612-3

Chapter 3

HARNESSING TECHNOLOGY THROUGH MOBILE LEARNING APPLICATIONS FOR MEDICAL INTERNS

Noi-Keng Koh[1], Barry J. Fraser[2,*] and Wai-Han Hoi[3]
[1]Curtin University, Singapore
[2]Curtin University, Australia
[3]National Healthcare Group, Singapore

ABSTRACT

To provide convenient learning-on-the-go professional development to busy medical interns, a team of senior medical consultant-instructors implemented mobile learning applications in an endocrinology unit at a teaching hospital in Singapore. This chapter describes the development, implementation and evaluation of a mixed-mode delivery method involving a well-designed user interface and user experience and mobile learning applications. Our mixed-methods evaluation involved qualitative observations and focus-group interviews, together with a quantitative survey for gathering interns' opinions about the levels of satisfaction,

* Corresponding Author's E-mail: B.Fraser@curtin.edu.au.

personal relevance and self-efficacy that they experienced with the professional development. Overall, the focus group-interviews revealed satisfaction among most participants, while the questionnaire data attested to the success of the program in fostering interns' self-efficacy. The future potential of using mobile learning applications as alternative learning-on-the-go solutions for busy medical practitioners is discussed.

Keywords: attitudes, evaluation, focus groups, medical interns, mixed methods, mobile learning applications, professional development, Singapore, technology

INTRODUCTION

In this chapter, we describe how we developed and implemented professional development courses for junior doctors involving use of mobile learning applications (Apps) in conjunction with face-to-face sessions with the senior doctors. This App provides seamless learning through a mobile device and a way to capture learning progress and provide diagnostic information for senior doctors for scaffolding and follow-up mentoring. We created a platform with a user-friendly dashboard and interesting learning opportunities for building a learning culture in a seamless, easy-to-use, intuitive and convenient manner for effective incidental learning, as well as quick sharing and dissemination of useful and bite-size information.

In the courses developed for interns, learning experiences were intense, varied and rich in opportunities for learning through mentoring. Associated challenges included how to structure learning courses to provide a rich learning environment for professional exchange (i.e., how to capture learning and build a learning culture within these professional communities of practice).

Development and implementation of 4 training sessions for interns at the hospital involved: 4 senior doctors in a core team; another 8 senior doctors who were observed/shadowed by the investigators; and 4 administrative staff members. In total, there were approximately 200 medical interns who participated in the training.

Furthermore, we conducted a mixed-methods evaluation of the program. The qualitative part of the evaluation involved informal observations during four professional development sessions, informal discussions with senior doctors and interns, and 3 focus-group interviews with 23 interns. The quantitative part of the evaluation involved an online survey for which 168 interns provided complete and valid responses.

DEVELOPMENT AND IMPLEMENTATION OF LEARNING MATERIALS

To identify the current training plans for resident doctors and conduct a training/learning gap analysis aimed at bridging the training gap, possible solutions were explored based on fact-finding through observations, hospital ward rounds, supervision clinic discourse and interviews with senior doctors, junior doctors and support staff. Our project initially involved conducting a training and learning needs analysis involving resident doctors in order to build pedagogically-sound teaching and learning platforms for them. This was followed by developing a learning trail for two modules as examples of how resident doctors could be more engaged in learning.

The ways in which teaching and learning take place influence students' approach to learning, but many medical schools could hinder rather than assist the development of the desired approach. The literature reviewed here suggests that bridging the gap requires not only substantial changes in the teaching, curriculum and, particularly, assessment, but also a new strategy based on identifying and assisting individual students whose preferred learning styles might not be consistent with traditional approaches.

Learning Framework

A simple model of the teaching–learning process was implemented through a multi-modal design in which every junior doctor was given an opportunity to learn from a senior doctor in varied workplace scenarios. Cognizant of the fact that different students learn in different ways, which is attributable partly to their preferred learning style and partly to the context in which the learning takes place, senior doctors could be observed transferring their knowledge, skills and expertise through various means. While some senior doctors attempted mixed-mode delivery involving role-play, inquiry and authentic case studies, others provided scaffolding through inquiry and problem-based approaches.

One of the challenges facing education in the information-age of the 21st century is the changing nature of work (Watkins, 2005). Experiential learning theory, which has played an important role in the development of educational practices, consists of the concrete-experience elements of observation, reflection and formation of abstract concepts, but not necessarily in that order (Kolb & Fry, 1975). McCarthy and McCarthy (2006) claim that theory alone cannot replace learning through experiential activities, which provide students with direct personal encounters and concrete experience. Kolb and Fry (1975) identified numerous examples of experience alone being insufficient for meeting particular learning goals, suggesting that experience should be complemented with exercises involving thinking, discussing or creatively processing experience-related cognitions and emotions.

Shulman (1988) suggests that reflective practice is what learners do when they look back at teaching and learning that have occurred and reconstruct, re-enact or recapture events, emotions and accomplishments. Reflective practice is a mode that integrates or links thought and action with reflection, involving thinking about and critically analysing one's actions with the goal of improving professional practice. Engaging in reflective practice requires individuals to assume the perspective of an external observer in order to identify the assumptions and feelings underlying their practice and then reflect on them.

Many students, when they experience active learning and shared inquiry, develop pro-social skills and positive emotions towards learning a subject. In classrooms that operate as learning communities, social and learning purposes advance together through all participants being involved and engaged in building knowledge (King & Watkins, 2012). Similarly, using authentic learning in the Retail Experience for Active Learning (REAL) project, Koh (2015) found that the project continued for many years because it was considered to be impactful and meaningful.

Students' observation and reflection upon these practical experiences and feedback from their workplace mentors can lead to the formation of new abstract concepts, which can then be tried out again in another situation, creating new experiences for students (Kolb, 1984). When students are placed in real-world environments with the autonomy to explore in structured and monitored ways, they operate within their Zone of Proximal Development (ZPD) (Vygotsky, 1978) in ways consistent with Lave and Wenger's (1991) notion of situated learning and legitimate peripheral participation and socialization of newcomers into practice. While in their ZPD, learners can strive towards the next level of awareness through independent problem solving of real-world issues, with guidance from their supervisors and workplace mentors or in collaboration with more-capable peers such as their colleagues.

The mixed-mode delivery model embraces a wide variety of teaching methods including cooperative learning, case studies, team-based learning, problem-based learning and strategies that are ICT-based, such as mobile applications, mind-tools, e-learning, video vignettes, online games and internet-based discussion forums. There are class dynamics and teaching and learning styles that are different from traditional teaching methods, as well as authentic and purposeful tasks to bridge the gap between theoretical content and the real world of work (Rainer & Matthews 2002). Andrews, Garrison and Magnusson's (1996) interviews about teaching excellence at the tertiary level revealed that excellent teachers use self-reflection to develop formal or informal models for teaching within a particular context and then attempt to 'live the model'. These ideas are embedded in the mixed-mode delivery model.

Our work with medical interns involved learning sessions with a mixed-mode delivery pedagogical framework in practice. In addition to workplace-situated learning and e-learning (to capitalise on emerging technologies to meet the needs of different types of learners), there were some tutorials and team-based learning during hospital ward rounds. Such learner-centred, process-oriented and skills-focused approaches to teaching are considered effective, but how learning is captured? Was there reflective learning? Could there be more sharing of valuable information or revelations? As new technologies open up new opportunities, educators are seeking new ways to engage learners in meaningful learning by providing challenging and real-life tasks and capitalising on technology as a tool for learning and collaboration.

Mixed-mode delivery provides a pedagogical model for mixing and matching engaging teaching and learning strategies to meet the demands of learners. Basically, it involves a variety of constructivist approaches to teaching and learning for each activity, even if only for about 10 minutes or so before following up with another strategy or activity or mode of learning. Constructivists recognise that learning occurs not in a vacuum, but is embedded in a particular social setting or learning environment (Duit & Treagust, 1995; Treagust, Duit & Fraser, 1996). Mixed-mode delivery involves constructivist and student-centred learning.

The following models often are adopted by teachers as teaching and learning strategies:

- *Rotation model* – Students rotate on a fixed schedule or at the teacher's discretion among classroom-based learning modalities. The rotation includes at least one learning mode for online learning, with other modes possibly including team-based learning, full-class instruction or case studies. This was observed when residents were assigned to different postings and had varied exposure to various practices.
- *Station rotation* –This model was adopted by one of the instructors in a course on risk management. The session was conducted while students were toggled between learning modalities and, while it

should have included at least one online learning, it did not (other than doing a Google search on mobile telephones). Other modalities include activities such as small-group or full-class instruction, role play, demonstrations, individual tutoring and group discussion assignments.

- *Laboratory rotation* – In this rotation model, students within a given course rotate on a fixed schedule or at the teacher's discretion among locations on a brick-and-mortar campus: from hospital ward rounds to clinics to operating theatres to tutorials At least one of these spaces is a learning laboratory for different learning modalities. The laboratory rotation model differs from the station rotation model in that students rotate among locations on the campus instead of staying in one classroom
- *Observation clinics* – In this powerful apprenticeship scheme model, junior doctors observe their mentors and later are observed by their mentors. This approach was tried out in one of the clinics and it is widely used in other medical learning environments.

Observations and Insights

During the implementation of our curriculum for medical residents, multi-modalities for teaching and learning were observed. As well as formal tutorials, hands-on workshops encompassed information literacy and risk management and ward rounds and clinics were intense and useful. On-the-job training and just-in-time learning during ward rounds were highly valued by junior doctors. During these sessions, the team presented a case and the senior doctor guided junior doctors through the thought processes. These processes were documented using a laptop computer that has a systematic template for reporting and can store data in a portal that is accessible to others for follow-up. The follow-up after hospital ward rounds provided impactful debriefing session in which junior doctors obtained further clarifications. Informal chat groups using Whatsapp–Debrief over a cup of tea/coffee at a cafe, Whatsapp chats using a telephone or laptop computer, and physical face-to-face sharing over lunch all were integral parts of the whole learning process. The teaching/learning modes involved were:

- Workshops (Risk Management)
- Supervision clinics (Endocrinology)
- Hands-on lectures (Information Literacy)
- e-learning followed by face-to-face sessions
- Ward rounds (Medicine and Surgery)
- Tutorials.

Common threads across the above learning modes were coaching or mentoring by a senior doctor and peer tutoring. Apprenticeship is a system for training a new generation of practitioners on a structured competency-based set of skills. Apprenticeships ranged from craft occupations or trades to professional licences to practice in a regulated profession.

Many of the original examples from Lave and Wenger (1991) were about adult learners for whom situated learning still has a particular resonance. For example, Hansman (2008) shows how adult learners discover, shape and make explicit their own knowledge through situated learning within a community of practice. First suggested by Lave and Wenger (1991) as a model of learning in a community of practice, situated learning allows individual students/learners to learn by socialization, visualization and imitation.

During hospital ward rounds, senior doctors stimulated learning by asking questions. Learning begins with people trying to solve problems (Hung, 2002). When learning is *problem based,* people explore real-life situations to find answers or solve problems. Hung highlights the importance of social aspects for learning, with learners gravitating to communities with shared interests to benefit from more-knowledgeable people. Hence, a community of practice is useful through virtual meetings such as WhatsApp, Google Meet, Zoom or Skype.

Team-based learning in practice at the hospital provided social experiences for members to work on cases and discuss these authentic experiences. When junior doctors are thrown into these real-life situations, they are compelled to learn. Therefore, by tackling the issues on hand, this team-based learning approach to designing curriculum lifts learners to a higher level of thinking (Hung, 2002), which happened sporadically during ward rounds, face-to-face tutorials, sessions in operating theatres and supervision clinics.

The resident interns in the endocrinology unit in our study had supervision clinics in which senior doctors were available for consultation and observing clinic sessions. A lot of learning was observed as junior doctors not only clarified and confirmed prescriptions and patient care and management, but also engaged in rigorous discussion of different scenarios requiring different treatments.

As well as clinical consultations, constructive dialogue among doctors is needed to address possible blind spots. Sometimes doctors even have to 'build stakeholder alliances' with caregivers to persuade and promote consensus and action, as well as to manage and motivate patients to follow up to achieve better healthcare management for effective patient outcomes. Again, how are these documented? Technology is the answer.

Emphasis was on learning techniques with practical applications and a clear understanding of how the communication process works in order to equip doctors to better manage patients. While professional style is characterized by precision, clarity, conciseness, directness, simplicity of language and logical flow, sometimes doctors are caught in situations in which their conscious efforts to show interest and adopt patient-centredness are exploited. For example, when one clinical consultation ended, there was a delay that led to an unnecessarily long wait for other patients. Therefore, balancing between time management and handling patients well requires skills beyond 'common sense'. There is a lack of structured learning, mentoring and documentation for authentic learning processes and acquisition of on-the-job skills. A seamless learning environment for capturing these authentic experiences would help to prevent reinventing the wheel.

For e-learning, the learning management system currently in use is Black Board. Junior doctors confessed that they prefer not to have to access courses through Black Board and still prefer face-to-face sessions. Reasons included that the technology was cumbersome to access because single sign-on is not possible, the interface was boring, and having no protected time for such activities impinged on their own scarce time. Tools such as self-marking quizzes and back-end analytics of learning provide better monitoring and assessment of learning.

The pedagogy of *seamless learning environments* is evolving, but it can only succeed if there are interactions and a community of practice. Sometimes, this involves interacting with a rich technological environment (e.g., blended learning, gamified app) or interacting with other people by means of a computer network. The pedagogy of successful e-learning echoes the apprenticeship model's individualized tasks for learners and guidance and feedback as they work (Halverson, 2009). The new generation of learners tends to respond better to bite-size amounts of information which spur them on to read more when they find topics interesting and relevant. Enhancements through virtual reality and augmented reality provided good hands-on activities for facilitating learning for every learner, compared with the limited resources associated with using real specimens.

Situated learning is becoming more involved with technology to help individuals learn differently from in the past. The model of learning a skill through technology mimics how individuals learned in the past from a professional person. Previously, when individuals learned about a particular topic, it was undertaken in person in a hands-on environment. Technology makes it possible to do these same things using a computer or any other mobile device. Interaction between individuals through the computer is another way to make situated learning more successful, as well as to give students an opportunity to have another way to learn.

While it is undeniable that there was learning taking place at each of these encounters, nagging questions are:

- When and where does learning take place?
- How do we evaluate if learning has taken place?
- How do we capture learning?

- How do we ensure that valuable knowledge and skills are shared?
- Can we create more opportunities for learning to take place more effectively? More engaging? Faster? More outreach?

In this study, some tools that could be part of transforming continuing education were used:

- A mobile application for online learning provided a convenient learning-on-the-go, user-friendly and well-organised learning journey.
- A platform for integrated learning and knowledge building brought together a professional community of learners through a thoughtful and well-designed dashboard.

Mixed-Methods Evaluation

Our evaluation of the professional development program for medical interns involved a mixed-methods approach (Creswell & Plano Clark, 2011). The qualitative component of the evaluation involved, among other elements, several focus-group interviews involving 23 interns. The quantitative part of the evaluation involved 168 interns responding to an online survey assessing the three constructs of satisfaction, personal relevance and self-efficacy.

Qualitative Methods and Results

In addition to our informal observations in the hospital and informal discussions with senior doctors and medical interns, we conducted three separate focus-group interviews (Hennink, 2007) involving 23 medical interns. These focus groups allowed interns to express their opinions with their peers in a comfortable social setting.

Focus-group discussions generally revealed positive opinions about the course among both instructors and interns because the time usually spent in lectures was freed up and because interns could study at their own pace and at times that best suited them. Discussions in face-to-face meetings were considered to be richer than in traditional lectures and tutorials because participants had previously studied the material in their own time.

Our evaluation revealed a good match between the wish lists of senior doctors and junior doctors, who both recognized the importance of situated learning for allowing interns to immediately apply what they've learned in the context of performing job-related tasks. Interaction between individuals through a computer or a mobile application is one way to make situated learning more successful, as well as providing students with another way to learn.

Senior doctors claimed that they would like more resident and junior doctors 'reading around' issues faced and thinking deeply about branching out into various other scenarios. With Amazon, a book selected triggers the artificial intelligence behind it and suggests other similar books. Likewise, will e-learning modules have enough built-in capability to arouse curiosity to read around an issue or a new learning point? While not every learner is on the same level playing field, it is everyone's wish to have access to more information and experiences. Moreover, problem-solving and the generation of new ideas can be better supported in a social learning environment where all of stakeholders experience the positive effects of ongoing learning, sharing and bringing rigour to discussions. Chat to learn?

Leveraging on the affordances of technology and deploying ICT tools for engaging learners already have changed the way in which we live and work. Traditional methods of staying up to date with medical knowledge include structured activities such as attending conferences and unstructured activities such as reading journals, both of which involve the unidirectional transfer of knowledge. While these remain relevant and useful, they can be beneficially augmented by leveraging on information and communication technology.

Halverson (2009) noted that computer simulations can create environments in which target skills are needed to solve engaging problems.

When situated learning is not possible, simulations can offer an alternative way to provide junior doctors with authentic learning experiences. Virtual reality and augmented reality are useful alternatives. Simulating the experiences that those learners would have while performing the functions required on-the-job allows the immediate application of what has been learned and benefit from an organization's existing knowledge base.

With recent advances in technology, it is possible to facilitate the social aspects of learning by virtually connecting individuals within a distributed community of practice in the online environment. Halverson (2009) notes that learners not only respond by feeding back information, but also they actively use their knowledge to explore, negotiate, interpret and create.

To this end, just as we build Wikipedia or use Google sites, any collaboration platform that has these affordances can promote a learning culture. How many junior doctors, as well as senior doctors, are using Whatsapp without instructions? The intuitive use of such a platform for immediate exchange of information and interaction serves its purpose and its ease of use and access makes it a very popular tool on mobile telephones. It is highly recommended, therefore, that the National Healthcare Group in Singapore provides such a platform so that hospital residents can interact and build on their repertoires of knowledge and skills by capturing information and proliferating it amongst this networked learning community.

Thus, we recommend the provision of a platform for this community for analyzing, remixing, co-creating and sharing the best and most-relevant content online for their own learning. Therefore, we should leverage on the affordances of technology to serve professional needs.

Quantitative Methods and Results

Our quantitative evaluation of the professional development course involving mobile applications made use of a questionnaire assessing medical interns' attitudes. In consultation with senior doctors, we identified three pertinent attitude scales for inclusion in our questionnaire: Satisfaction, Personal Relevance and Self-Efficacy.

The Satisfaction (or enjoyment) scale is based on items adapted from the Test of Science Related Attitudes (Fraser, 1981). The Personal Relevance scale, which assesses the extent to which participants perceive the course as being personally relevant to their daily work and study, is adapted from the Constructivist Learning Environment Survey (Koh & Fraser, 2014a; Taylor, Fraser & Fisher, 1997). The Self-Efficacy scale is adapted from Koh and Fraser (2014b) and assesses residents' feelings of confidence in handling work situations at the hospital. A sample item for each of these three scales is provided in Table 1.

A total of 168 medical interns who had participated in the course provided complete and valid responses to an online administration of our questionnaire. In total, the questionnaire contains 17 items (5 items each in Satisfaction and Personal Relevance and 7 items in Self-Efficacy).

When we checked the reliability of each questionnaire scale by calculating Cronbach's alpha coefficient, scale reliabilities were found to range from 0.86 to 0.94 (see Table 1), which indicates strong reliability. We also checked the structure of our three-scale questionnaire by conducting factor analysis (principal axis with oblimin rotation and Kaiser normalization) for the responses from 168 medical residents. All 17 questionnaire items had a factor loading above 0.5 on its own scale and no other scale, all eigenvalues were larger than 1.0, and the total proportion of variance explained was 61.7%. The results support our questionnaire's three-scale structure.

Table 1. Sample item, reliability, descriptive statistics and difference between two times (number of standard deviations and statistical significance)

Scale	Sample Item	No of Items	Reliability	Mean		SD		Difference	
				Time 1	Time 2	Time 1	Time 2	No. of SDs	Significant
Satisfaction	I enjoy activities in this module.	5	0.91	3.77	3.99	0.59	0.60	0.37	Yes
Personal Relevance	My new learning starts with problems/issues about the real patient environment.	5	0.87	4.20	4.28	0.51	0.45	0.19	Yes
Self-Efficacy	I am confident in handling patients with hypocortisolism.	7	0.94	3.49	4.11	0.69	0.52	1.02	Yes

Sample size = 168.

Our evaluation design mainly involved comparing questionnaire scale scores near the beginning of curriculum implementation (Time 1 or pretest) and after the study had been in progress for several months (Time 2 or posttest). These differences in scores between Time 1 and Time 2 for each scale are reported in Table 1 in terms of their magnitudes (or effect sizes, Cohen, 1988) expressed in standard deviations, as well as their statistical significance ($p < 0.05$) based on t tests. (Because pretest information was not available for Personal Relevance, we compared interns' scores at Time 2 with a comparable control group of doctors following traditional instructional methods.)

According to Table 1, differences between scores at the two different times were statistically significant ($p< 0.05$) for each of the three questionnaire scales, but the magnitude of these differences varied between the three scales. The difference was small for Personal Relevance (0.19 standard deviations), modest for Satisfaction (0.37 standard deviations) and large for Self-Efficacy (1.02 standard deviations) according to Cohen's (1988) criteria. For each of the three scales, the direction of the changes in Table 1 supports the effectiveness of the curriculum involving mobile applications, with the large improvement in students' self-efficacy being especially noteworthy.

CONCLUSION

In this chapter, we described how we collaborated with a dozen senior doctors at a teaching hospital in Singapore in designing and implementing professional development experiences involving approximately 200 medical interns and the use of mobile learning applications (Apps). We also conducted a mixed-methods evaluation involving qualitative observations and focus-group interviews and a quantitative questionnaire survey. Three focus-group interviews with 23 interns attested to predominantly positive opinions about the course, whereas questionnaire responses from 168 interns supported the success of the program in fostering their self-efficacy.

With recent advances in technology, it is possible to facilitate social aspects of learning by virtually connecting individuals within a distributed community of practice in online environments. According to Halverson (2009), learners not only respond by feeding back information, but they also actively use what they know to interpret, create and construct solutions in the process of learning. As medical schools shift to more collaborative models of training in which students are encouraged to discuss and challenge what they are taught, we doubt that traditional learning approaches will be ideal for future generations of clinicians.

Fortunately, emerging tools can add a new dimension to continuing education in which primary care physicians can participate in thoughtful debates about the latest hypertension guidelines with peers who are not necessarily co-located at the same physical workplace.

References

Andrews, J., Garrison, D. R., & Magnusson, K. (1996). The teaching and learning transaction in higher education: A study of excellent professors and their students. *Teaching in Higher Education, 1*(1), 81-103.

Cohen, J. (1988). *Statistical power analysis for the behavioral sciences*. Hillsdale, NJ: Erlbaum.

Creswell, J.W., & Plano Clark, V.L. (2011). *Designing and conducting mixed methods research* (2nd ed.). London: Sage.

Duit R., & Treagust D.F. (1995). Students' conceptions and constructivist teaching approaches. In B.J. Fraser and H.J. Walberg (Eds.), *Improving science education* (pp. 46-49.) Chicago: National Society for the Study of Education.

Fraser, B.J. (1981). *Test of Science Related Attitudes.* Melbourne: Australian Council for Educational Research.

Halverson, A. C. (2009). *Rethinking education in the age of technology*. New York: Teachers College Press.

Hansman, C. (2008). Adult learning in communities of practice: Situating theory in practice. In C. Kimble and P. Hildreth (Ed.), *Communities of practice: Creating learning environments for educators* (Vol. 1, pp. 293-310). Charlotte, NC: Information Age Publishing.

Hennink, M.M. (2007). *International focus group research: A handbook for the health and social sciences*. Cambridge, UK: Cambridge University Press.

Hung, D. (2002). Situated cognition and problem-based learning: Implications for learning and instruction with technology. *Journal of Interactive Learning Research, 13*(4), 393-415.

King, R. B., & Watkins, D. A. (2012). "Socializing" achievement goal theory: The need for social goals. *Psychological Studies*, *57*(1), 112-116.

Koh, N.K., & Fraser, B.J. (2014a). Learning environment associated with use of mixed mode delivery model among secondary business studies students in Singapore. *Learning Environments Research, 17*(2), 157-171.

Koh, N.K., & Fraser, B.J. (2014b). Determinants of financial attitudes among secondary-school students in Singapore. *World Studies in Education, 15*(2), 41-52.

Koh, N. K. (2015). The Retail Experience for Active Learning (REAL) experience). In Y. H. Cho, I. S. Caleon and M. Kapur (Eds.), *Authentic problem solving and learning for the 21st century* (pp. 200-210). Singapore: Springer.

Kolb, D. A. (1984). *Experiential learning: Experience as the source of learning and development.* Englewood Cliffs, NJ: Prentice Hall.

Kolb, D. A., & Fry, R. (1975). Towards an applied theory of experiential learning. In C. L. Cooper (Ed.), *Theories of group process*. London: Wiley.

Lave, J., & Wenger, E. (1991). *Situated learning. Legitimate peripheral participation.* Cambridge: University of Cambridge Press.

McCarthy, B., & McCarthy, D. (2006). *Teaching around the 4MAT cycle: Designing instruction for diverse learners with diverse learning styles.* Thousand Oaks, CA: Corwin.

Rainer, J., & Matthews, M. (2002). Ownership of learning in teacher education. *Action in Teacher Education, 24*, 22-30.

Shulman, L. S. (1988). Teaching alone, learning together: Needed agenda for new reforms. In T. J. Sergiovanni and J. H. Moore (Eds.), *Schooling for tomorrow: Directing reforms to issues that count.* Boston: Allyn & Bacon.

Taylor, P.C., Fraser, B.J., & Fisher, D.L. (1997). Monitoring constructivist classroom learning environments. *International Journal of Educational Research, 27,* 293-302.

Treagust, D.F., Duit, R., & Fraser, B.J. (1996). Overview: Research on students' preinstructional conceptions – the driving force for improving teaching and learning in science and mathematics. In D.F. Treagust, R. Duit and B.J. Fraser (Eds.), *Improving teaching and learning in science and mathematics.* New York: Teachers College Press.

Vygotsky, L. (1978). Apprentissage et developpement a l'age prescolaire. *Societe Francaise, 52*(2), 35-45. [Preschool learning and development. *French society*]

Watkins, R. (2005). Developing interactive e-learning activities. *Performance Improvement, 44*(5), 5-7.

In: Computers in Education
Editor: Ganelon Metivier
ISBN: 978-1-53618-612-3

Chapter 4

DESIGN OF NONLINEAR TWO-DIMENSIONAL INTEGRAL CALCULATOR FOR MATHEMATICS AND ENGINEERING EDUCATION

Çiğdem Dinçkal*
Department of Civil Engineering, Çankaya University, Ankara, Turkey

ABSTRACT

Two-dimensional (2D) integration of any function with two independent variables is one of the substantial parts of the solution for many problems in mathematics and engineering education. Due to the complexity of function to be integrated, most of these 2D integrals cannot be calculated analytically. So the demand for numerical integration techniques and design of calculators based on these techniques increase. For these reasons, this chapter presents some implementations of Newton-Cotes integration methods (such as Simpson's 1/3, Composite Trapezoidal, Composite Simpson's 1/3, and Boole's rules) to nonlinear 2D integrals with a new calculator: TWOD_integral_calculator designed

* Corresponding Author's E-mail: cdinckal@cankaya.edu.tr.

by the help of Matlab Graphical User Interface (GUI). This calculator is so user-friendly that any kind of users (educator, student) can employ it conveniently for any integral given. The computational speed and convergence of these methods are compared in terms of true percent relative error and the computation of elapsed and CPU time for various segments. True percent relative errror is also obtained for each method. If exact result is not known, TWOD_integral_calculator can perform only numerical computations without true percent relative error calculations. TWOD_integral_calculator is also tested for mathematics and engineering applications. The results for each application obtained from calculator are presented.

Keywords: TWOD_integral_calculator; Matlab GUI; Newton-Cotes closed integration methods; elapsed time; CPU time.

INTRODUCTION

As many science and engineering problems necessitate the solution of nonlinear two-dimensional integrals [7].

The following illustration is form of a 2D integral over a rectangular domain[c, d]×[a, b]:

$$I = \int_c^d \int_a^b f(x, y) dxdy \tag{1}$$

In Calculus, integral in Eq. (1) can be computed as iterated integral

$$\int_c^d \left(\int_a^b f(x, y) dx \right) dy = \int_a^b \left(\int_c^d f(x, y) dy \right) dx \tag{2}$$

The need of numerical integration of 2D integrals arises in many mathematical models, as most of these integrals cannot be evaluated analytically [1, 2, 5, 14, 16, 18]. Any numerical integration technique is based on the idea of iterated integral.

Furthermore, extensive researches have taken place to evaluate 2D and higher dimensional integrals numerically with use of generated computer codes [2-6, 8, 9, 11-13, 15-23, 26-30]. Some Newton-Cotes closed integration methods are employed and developed in these studies. Also certain works have employed some Newton-Cotes formulations to solve science and engineering problems involving integrations [10, 24, 25, 29]. Main aim of this chapter is to design user-friendly calculator called as TWOD_integral_calculator which solves any nonlinear 2D integrals numerically by use of Matlab GUI for the first time in literature. The algorithm behind this calculator is based on Newton-Cotes closed integration techniques (such as Simpson's 1/3 rule, Composite Trapezoidal rule, Composite Simpson's 1/3 rule, and Boole's rule), simultaneously.

TWOD_integral_calculator performs computation of elapsed and CPU time and also convergence of each method in terms of true percent relative error for various segments. If user does not enter exact result into the related box, TWOD_integral_calculator can only solve integrals numerically without true percent relative error calculations.

METHODS

The well-known Newton-Cotes integration methods are employed such that these methods are adopted for multi-dimensional integration in some straight-forward following methods.

For all methods: $y_j = c + jh_y$, $j = 0,1,2, \ldots \ldots . n_y$, and $x_i = a + ih_x$, $i = 0,1,2, \ldots \ldots . n_x$.

Simpson's 1/3 Rule Formulation

Applications of the formulation to the integration in y by treating x as a constant yield the following expression:

$$\int_c^d f(x,y)\,dy = \frac{h_y}{3}[f(x,y_1) + f(x,y_3) + 4f(x,y_2)] - \frac{h_y^5}{90}\frac{\partial^4 f(x,\mu_y)}{\partial y^4} \quad (3)$$

For some $\mu_y \in [c,d]$.

Then application of the method to the integral in the x- coordinate:

$$\int_a^b \int_c^d f(x,y)dy\,dx = \frac{h_y}{3}\left[\int_a^b f(x,y_0)dx + 4\int_a^b f(x,y_1)dx + \int_a^b f(x,y_2)dx\right] - \frac{h_y^5}{90}\int_a^b \frac{\partial^4 f(x,\mu_y)}{\partial y^4}dx \quad (4)$$

Simply implementation of this method in the x-coordinate, for each integral in the expression gives:

$$\int_a^b \int_c^d f(x,y)dy\,dx \approx \frac{h_y}{3}\left\{\frac{h_x}{3}[f(x_0,y_0) + f(x_1,y_0) + 4f(x_2,y_0)] - \frac{h_x^5}{90}\frac{\partial^4 f(\mu_x,y)}{\partial x^4} + 4\left[\frac{h_x}{3}\begin{bmatrix} f(x_0,y_1) + f(x_1,y_1) + \\ 4f(x_2,y_1) \end{bmatrix} - \frac{h_x^5}{90}\frac{\partial^4 f(\mu_x,y)}{\partial x^4}\right] + \frac{h_x}{3}[f(x_0,y_2) + f(x_1,y_2) + 4f(x_2,y_2)] - \frac{h_x^5}{90}\frac{\partial^4 f(\mu_x,y)}{\partial x^4}\right\} - \frac{(b-a)h_y^5}{90}\frac{\partial^4 f(x,\mu_y)}{\partial y^4} \quad (5)$$

From Eq. (5), the error for the method is derived as

$$E = -\left[\frac{(d-c)h_x^5 \partial^4 f(v_x,\mu_x)}{90\partial x^4} + \frac{(b-a)h_y^5 \partial^4 f(v_y,\mu_y)}{90\partial y^4}\right] \quad (6)$$

For some (v_x,μ_x), $(v_y,\mu_y) \in R = [a,b] \times [c,d]$.

Composite Trapezoidal Rule Formulation

Implementation of Composite Trapezoidal rule to the integration in y by treating x as a constant gives the following expression:

$$\int_c^d f(x,y)\,dy = \frac{h_y}{2}\left[f(x,y_0) - f(x,y_n) + \sum_{j=1}^{n_y-1}[2f(x,y_j)]\right] - \frac{(d-c)h_y^2}{12}\frac{\partial^2 f(x,\mu_y)}{\partial y^2} \quad (7)$$

For some $\mu_y \in [c,d]$.

Then application of the method to the integral in the x- coordinate:

$$\int_a^b \int_c^d f(x,y)dy\,dx = \frac{h_y}{2}\Big[\int_a^b f(x,y_0)dx - \int_a^b f(x,y_n)dx + \sum_{j=1}^{n_y-1}\Big[2\int_a^b f(x,y_j)dx\Big]\Big] - \frac{(d-c)h_y^2}{12}\int_a^b \frac{\partial^2 f(x,\mu_y)}{\partial y^2}dx \tag{8}$$

Simply execution of Composite Trapezoidal rule in the x-coordinate, for each integral in the expression takes the following form:

$$\int_a^b \int_c^d f(x,y)dy\,dx \approx \frac{h_y}{2}\Big\{\frac{h_x}{2}[f(x_0,y_0) - f(x_n,y_0) + \sum_{i=1}^{n_x-1}(2f(x_i,y_0))] - \frac{(b-a)h_x^2}{12}\frac{\partial^2 f(\mu_x,y)}{\partial x^2} - \frac{h_x}{2}[f(x_0,y_n) - f(x_n,y_n) + \sum_{i=1}^{n_x-1}(2f(x_i,y_n))] + \frac{(b-a)h_x^2}{12}\frac{\partial^2 f(\mu_x,y)}{\partial x^2} + \frac{h_x}{2}\sum_{j=1}^{n_y-1} 2\Big[f(x_0,y_j) - f(x_n,y_j) + \sum_{i=1}^{n_x-1}\big(2f(x_i,y_j)\big) - \frac{(b-a)h_x^2}{12}\frac{\partial^2 f(\mu_x,y)}{\partial x^2}\Big]\Big\} - \frac{(d-c)(b-a)h_y^2}{12}\frac{\partial^2 f(x,\mu_y)}{\partial y^2} \tag{9}$$

From Eq. (9), the error for Composite Trapezoidal rule formulation is derived as

$$E = -\frac{(b-a)(d-c)}{12}\Big[\frac{h_x^2\partial^2 f(\nu_x,\mu_x)}{\partial x^2} + \frac{h_y^2\partial^2 f(\nu_y,\mu_y)}{\partial y^2}\Big] \tag{10}$$

For some (ν_x,μ_x), $(\nu_y,\mu_y) \in R = [a,b]\times[c,d]$.

Composite Simpson's 1/3 Rule Formulation

Implementation of this method to the integration in y by treating x as a constant yields the following expression:

$$\int_c^d f(x,y)\,dy = \frac{h_y}{3}\Big[f(x,y_0) - f(x,y_n) + \sum_{j=1}^{\frac{n_y}{2}}[2f(x,y_{2j}) + 4f(x,y_{2j-1})]\Big] - \frac{(d-c)h_y^4}{180}\frac{\partial^4 f(x,\mu_y)}{\partial y^4} \tag{11}$$

For some $\mu_y \in [c, d]$

Then application of the method to the integral in the x- coordinate:

$$\int_a^b \int_c^d f(x,y)dy\,dx = \frac{h_y}{3}\left[\int_a^b f(x,y_0)dx - \int_a^b f(x,y_n)dx + \sum_{j=1}^{\frac{n_y}{2}}\left[2\int_a^b f(x,y_{2j})dx + 4\int_a^b f(x,y_{2j-1})dx\right]\right] - \frac{(d-c)h_y^4}{180}\int_a^b \frac{\partial^4 f(x,\mu_y)}{\partial y^4}dx \quad (12)$$

Simply application of Composite Simpson's 1/3 rule in the x-coordinate, for each integral in the expression yields:

$$\int_a^b \int_c^d f(x,y)dy\,dx \approx \frac{h_y}{3}\left\{\frac{h_x}{3}\left[f(x_0,y_0) - f(x_n,y_0) + \sum_{i=1}^{\frac{n_x}{2}}(2f(x_{2i},y_0) + 4f(x_{2i-1},y_0))\right] - \frac{(b-a)h_x^4}{180}\frac{\partial^4 f(\mu_x,y)}{\partial x^4} - \frac{h_x}{3}\left[f(x_0,y_n) - f(x_n,y_n) + \sum_{i=1}^{\frac{n_x}{2}}(2f(x_{2i},y_n) + 4f(x_{2i-1},y_n))\right] + \frac{(b-a)h_x^4}{180}\frac{\partial^4 f(\mu_x,y)}{\partial x^4} + \frac{h_x}{3}\sum_{j=1}^{\frac{n_y}{2}} 2\left[f(x_0,y_{2j}) - f(x_n,y_{2j}) + \sum_{i=1}^{\frac{n_x}{2}}\left(2f(x_{2i},y_{2j}) + 4f(x_{2i-1},y_{2j})\right) - \frac{(b-a)h_x^4}{180}\frac{\partial^4 f(\mu_x,y)}{\partial x^4}\right] + \frac{h_x}{3}\sum_{j=1}^{\frac{n_y}{2}} 4\left[f(x_0,y_{2j-1}) - f(x_n,y_{2j-1}) + \sum_{i=1}^{\frac{n_x}{2}}\left(2f(x_{2i},y_{2j-1}) + 4f(x_{2i-1},y_{2j-1})\right) - \frac{(b-a)h_x^4}{180}\frac{\partial^4 f(\mu_x,y)}{\partial x^4}\right]\right\} - \frac{(d-c)(b-a)h_y^4}{180}\frac{\partial^4 f(x,\mu_y)}{\partial y^4} \quad (13)$$

From Eq. (13), the error for Composite Simpson's 1/3 method is derived as

$$E = -\frac{(b-a)(d-c)}{180}\left[\frac{h_x^4 \partial^4 f(\nu_x,\mu_x)}{\partial x^4} + \frac{h_y^4 \partial^4 f(\nu_y,\mu_y)}{\partial y^4}\right] \quad (14)$$

For some $(\nu_x,\mu_x), (\nu_y,\mu_y) \in R = [a,b] \times [c,d]$.

Boole's Rule Formulation

Firstly, application of Boole's rule for 5 segments to the integration in y by treating x as constant yields the following expression:

$$\int_c^d f(x,y)\,dy = \frac{(d-c)}{288}[19 * f(x,y_0) + 75 * f(x,y_1) + 50 * f(x,y_2) + 50 * f(x,y_3) + 75 * f(x,y_4) + 19 * f(x,y_5)] - \frac{275h_y^7}{12096}\frac{\partial^6 f(x,\mu_y)}{\partial y^6} \quad (15)$$

For some $\mu_y \in [c,d]$.

Then application of Boole's rule for n=5 to the integral in the x-coordinate:

$$\int_a^b \int_c^d f(x,y)dy\,dx = \frac{(b-a)(d-c)}{288^2}\left[19\int_a^b f(x,y_0)dx + 75\int_a^b f(x,y_1)dx + 50\int_a^b f(x,y_2)dx + 50\int_a^b f(x,y_3)dx + 75\int_a^b f(x,y_4)dx + 19\int_a^b f(x,y_5)dx\right] - \frac{275h_y^7}{12096}\int_a^b \frac{\partial^6 f(x,\mu_y)}{\partial y^6}dx \quad (16)$$

Finally, the explicit result of the simply application of Boole's rule in the x-coordinate, for each integral in the expression gives:

$$\int_a^b \int_c^d f(x,y)dy\,dx \approx \frac{(b-a)(d-c)}{288^2}\Big\{19\Big[19f(x_0,y_0) + 75f(x_1,y_0) + 50f(x_2,y_0) + 50f(x_3,y_0) + 75f(x_4,y_0) + 19f(x_5,y_0) - \frac{275h_x^7}{12096}\frac{\partial^6 f(\mu_x,y)}{\partial x^6}\Big] + 75\Big[19f(x_0,y_1) + 75f(x_1,y_1) + 50f(x_2,y_1) + 50f(x_3,y_1) + 75f(x_4,y_1) + 19f(x_5,y_1) - \frac{275h_x^7}{12096}\frac{\partial^6 f(\mu_x,y)}{\partial x^6}\Big] + 50\Big[19f(x_0,y_2) + 75f(x_1,y_2) + 50f(x_2,y_2) + 50f(x_3,y_2) + 75f(x_4,y_2) + 19f(x_5,y_2) - \frac{275h_x^7}{12096}\frac{\partial^6 f(\mu_x,y)}{\partial x^6}\Big] + 50\Big[19f(x_0,y_3) + 75f(x_1,y_3) + 50f(x_2,y_3) + 50f(x_3,y_3) + 75f(x_4,y_3) + 19f(x_5,y_3) - \frac{275h_x^7}{12096}\frac{\partial^6 f(\mu_x,y)}{\partial x^6}\Big] + 75\Big[19f(x_0,y_4) + 75f(x_1,y_4) + 50f(x_2,y_4) + 50f(x_3,y_4) + 75f(x_4,y_4) + 19f(x_5,y_4) - \frac{275h_x^7}{12096}\frac{\partial^6 f(\mu_x,y)}{\partial x^6}\Big] + 19\Big[19f(x_0,y_5) + 75f(x_1,y_5) + 50f(x_2,y_5) + 50f(x_3,y_5) + 75f(x_4,y_5) + 19f(x_5,y_5) - \frac{275h_x^7}{12096}\frac{\partial^6 f(\mu_x,y)}{\partial x^6}\Big]\Big\} - \frac{275h_y^7}{12096}\frac{(b-a)\partial^6 f(x,\mu_y)}{\partial y^6} \quad (17)$$

From Eq. (17), the error for Boole's rule for 5 segments is found as

$$E = -(b-a)\left[\frac{275(d-c)h_x^7 \partial^6 f(v_x, \mu_x)}{3483648 \partial x^6} + \frac{h_y^7 \partial^6 f(v_y, \mu_y)}{12 \partial y^6}\right] \quad (18)$$

For some (v_x, μ_x), $(v_y, \mu_y) \in R = [a, b] \times [c, d]$.

NUMERICAL EXAMPLES

Numerical examples, error computations and computational speed for each method are presented in this section. All numerical examples are solved up to 500 segments (n = 500). TWOD_integral_calculator performs integration for any given integral with use of Simpson's 1/3, Composite Simpson's 1/3, Composite Trapezoidal and Boole's rule and error computation (if exact results are known) with CPU time and elapsed time calculations in MATLAB R2016a.

Example 1

To determine average temperature of an 8-m long (x dimension) and 6-m wide (y dimension) rectangular heated plate, the following 2D integral is required to be calculated [14].

$$\int_0^6 \int_0^8 (2xy + 2x - x^2 - 2y^2 + 72)\, dxdy \quad (19)$$

The exact (analytic) result is 2816.

The results of computation and true percent relative error (error: ε) of corresponding methods in case of n ≤ 5 are summarized in Table1 and Table 2, respectively:

Table 1. Computation results of example 1 for $n \leq 5$

n	Methods	Results
2	Composite Trapezoidal Rule	2544
	Simpson's 1/3 Rule	2816
4	Composite Trapezoidal Rule	2748
	Composite Simpson's 1/3 Rule	2816
5	Composite Trapezoidal Rule	2772.48
	Boole's Rule	2816

Table 2. Error computations of example 1 for $n \leq 5$

n	Methods	Results
2	Composite Trapezoidal Rule	9.6591
	Simpson's 1/3 Rule	0
4	Composite Trapezoidal Rule	2.4148
	Composite Simpson's 1/3 Rule	0
5	Composite Trapezoidal Rule	1.5455
	Boole's Rule	0

According to Table 1 and Table 2; analytic (true) results of the integral can be obtained by use of Simpson's 1/3 rule (when $n = 2$), Composite Simpson's 1/3 Rule (when $n = 4$) and Boole's rule (when $n = 5$).

The elapsed time and CPU time for the corresponding methods when $n \leq 5$ in MATLAB are presented in the following Tables:

Table 3. Elapsed time for computations of example 1 for $n \leq 5$

n	Methods	Results
2	Composite Trapezoidal Rule	0.011401
	Simpson's 1/3 Rule	0.011583
4	Composite Trapezoidal Rule	0.017856
	Composite Simpson's 1/3 Rule	0.02188
5	Composite Trapezoidal Rule	0.027246
	Boole's Rule	0.020125

Table 4. CPU time for computations of example 1 for $n \leq 5$

n	Methods	Results
2	Composite Trapezoidal Rule	0.031200
	Simpson's 1/3 Rule	0.000000
4	Composite Trapezoidal Rule	0.031200
	Composite Simpson's 1/3 Rule	0.156000
5	Composite Trapezoidal Rule	0.093601
	Boole's Rule	0.031200

To Table 3, elapsed time for Composite Trapezoidal Rule is the minimum among the other rules whereas CPU time for Simpson's 1/3 Rule is the minimum among the other methods in Table 4.

The results of computation and true percent relative error (ε) of related methods for n > 5 are illustrated in Figure 1 and Figure 2, respectively.

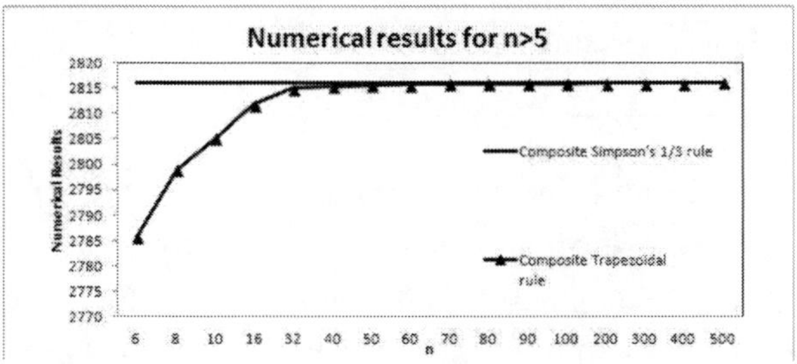

Figure 1. Computation results of example 1 for $n > 5$.

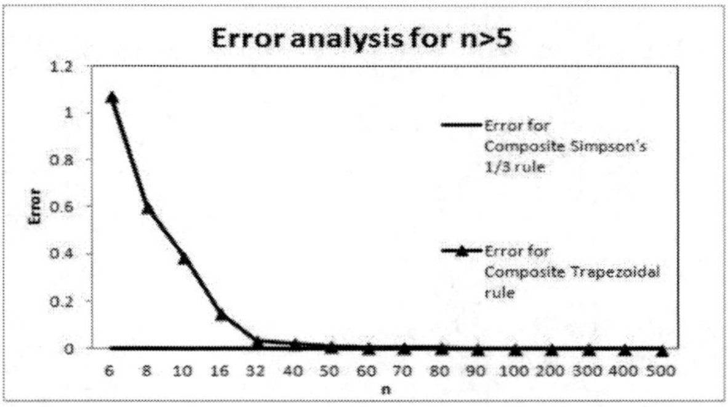

Figure 2. Error analysis of example 1 in case of n > 5.

As it is seen from both Figure 1 and Figure 2, Composite Trapezoidal method yields more error than Composite Simpson's 1/3 rule. Starting from $n = 6$ up to $n = 500$ the exact result is obtained by Composite Simpson's 1/3 rule. Contrary, when n starts from 50 to 500, Composite Trapezoidal rule yields the exact result.

Elapsed time and CPU time for computation of all segments up to 500 segments are plotted in Figure 3 and Figure 4, respectively.

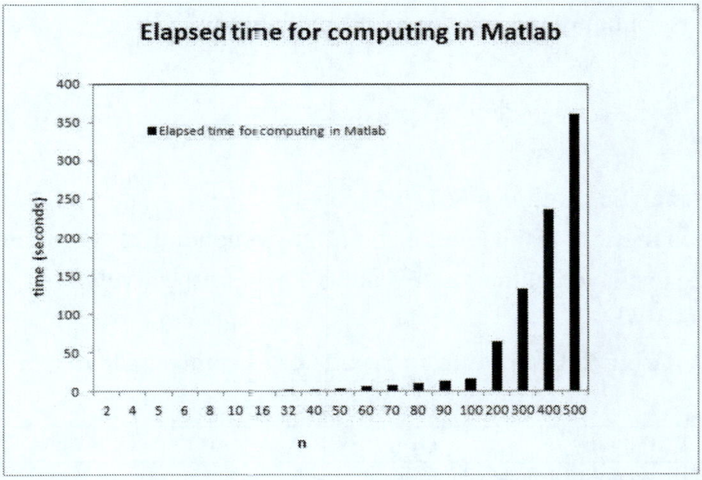

Figure 3. Elapsed time for computations (up to 500 segments) in example 1.

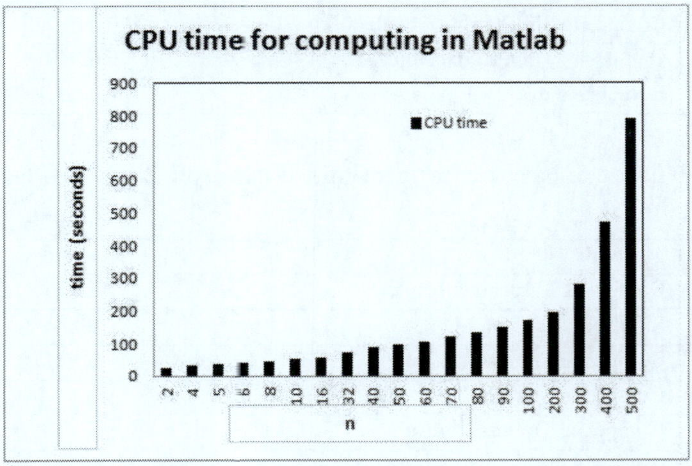

Figure 4. CPU time for computations (up to 500 segments) in example 1.

To Figure 3 and Figure 4, an increase in number of segments causes an increase in computation of elapsed and CPU time in MATLAB for example 1.

Example 2

The total work done by a force on a two-dimensional dynamics problem is found by solving the following integral [22].

$$\int_0^2 \int_0^1 (x^2 - 2xy + 3xy^2 + y^3)\, dxdy \qquad (20)$$

The analytic result is 6.667.

The numerical results and error of corresponding methods in case of $n \leq 5$ are displayed in the Table 5 and Table 6, respectively.

Table 5. Computation results of example 2 for $n \leq 5$

n	Methods	Results
2	Composite Trapezoidal Rule	8.250
	Simpson's 1/3 Rule	6.667
4	Composite Trapezoidal Rule	7.063
	Composite Simpson's 1/3 Rule	6.667
5	Composite Trapezoidal Rule	6.920
	Boole's Rule	6.667

Table 6. Error computations of example 2 for $n \leq 5$

n	Methods	Results
2	Composite Trapezoidal Rule	23.75
	Simpson's 1/3 Rule	0
4	Composite Trapezoidal Rule	5.9375
	Composite Simpson's 1/3 Rule	0
5	Composite Trapezoidal Rule	3.8
	Boole's Rule	0

According to Table 5 and Table 6, the computations by Simpson's 1/3 (when $n = 2$), Composite Simpson's 1/3 Rule (when $n = 4$) and Boole's rule (when $n = 5$) yield the exact result of the problem in example 2.

The elapsed time and CPU time in MATLAB for the corresponding methods when $n \leq 5$ are displayed in the Table 7 and Table 8 in terms of seconds, respectively.

Table 7. Elapsed time for computations of example 2 for $n \leq 5$

n	Methods	Results
2	Composite Trapezoidal Rule	0.03481
	Simpson's 1/3 Rule	0.01082
4	Composite Trapezoidal Rule	0.018386
	Composite Simpson's 1/3 Rule	0.034403
5	Composite Trapezoidal Rule	0.037091
	Boole's Rule	0.019111

Table 8. CPU time for computations of example 2 for $n \leq 5$

n	Methods	Results
2	Composite Trapezoidal Rule	0.015600
	Simpson's 1/3 Rule	0.0312
4	Composite Trapezoidal Rule	0.0312
	Composite Simpson's 1/3 Rule	0.1248
5	Composite Trapezoidal Rule	0.0624
	Boole's Rule	0.0312

To Table 7 and Table 8, the elapsed time for Simpson's 1/3 rule in MATLAB is the minimum among the other methods and CPU time for Composite Trapezoidal rule (when n = 2) is the minimum among the other rules for example 2.

The numerical results and true percent relative error (ε) of related methods for $n > 5$ are displayed in Figure 5 and Figure 6, respectively.

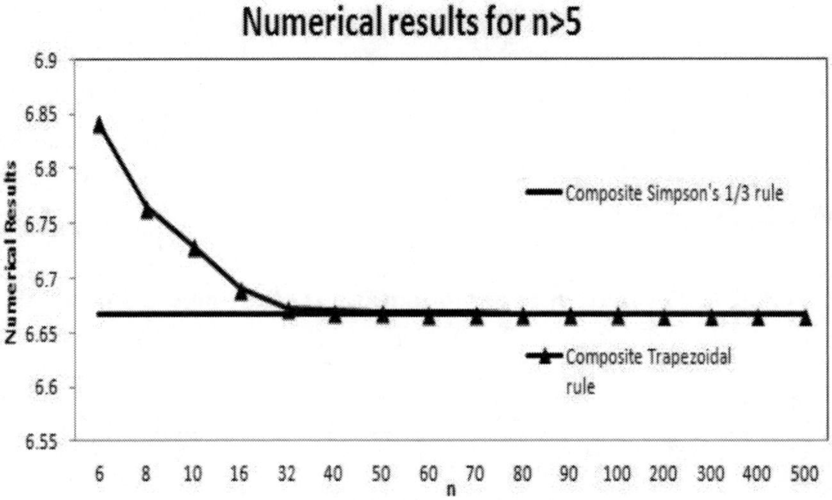

Figure 5. Computation results of example 2 for $n > 5$.

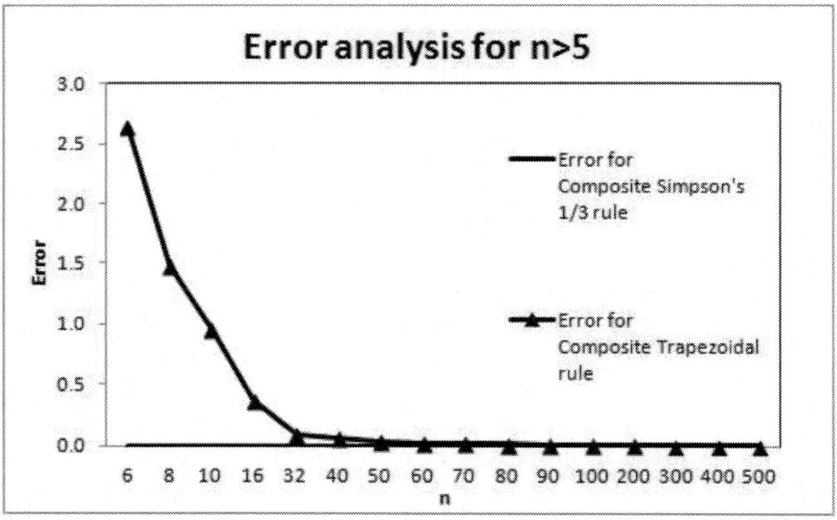

Figure 6. ε results of example 2 for n > 5.

As in both Figure 5 and Figure 6, Composite Trapezoidal method gives more error than Composite Simpson's 1/3 rule. When n = 50, the exact result is obtained by Composite Trapezoidal rule, simultaneously.

Elapsed time and CPU time for computation of all segments up to 500 segments are exhibited in Figure 7 and Figure 8, respectively.

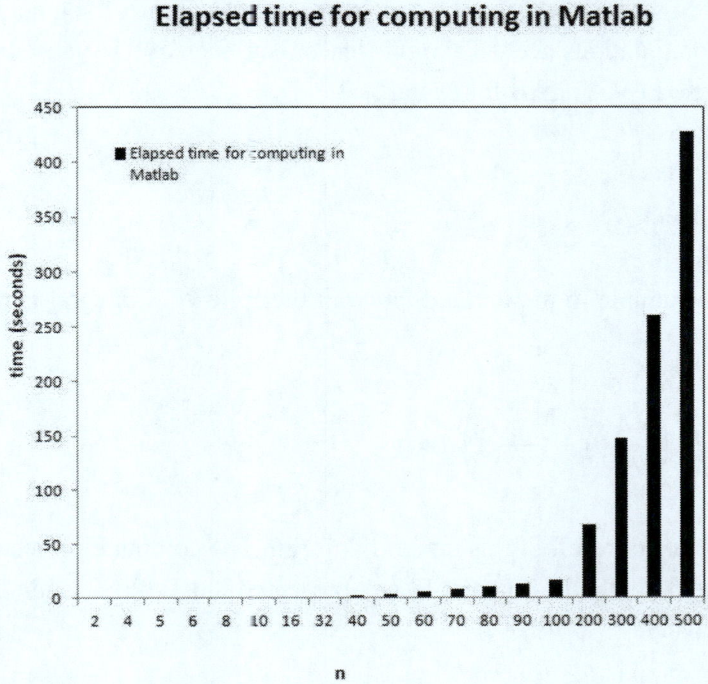

Figure 7. Elapsed time for computations (up to 500 segments) in example 2.

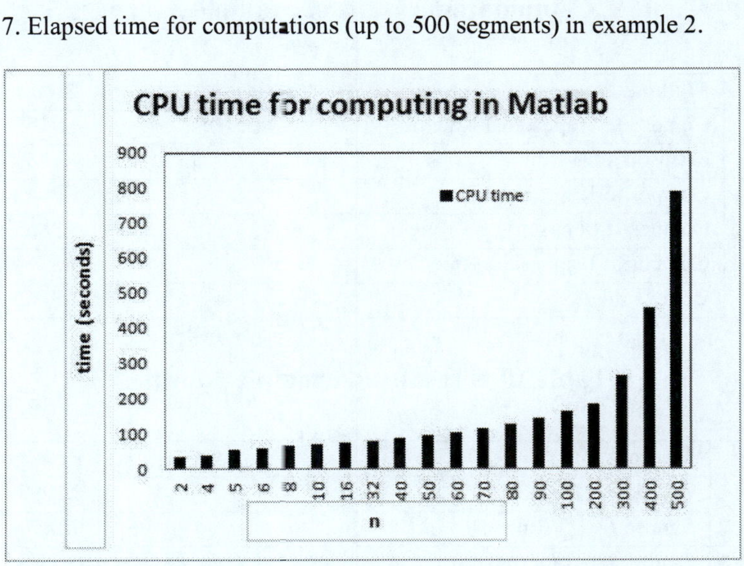

Figure 8. CPU time for computations (up to 500 segments) in example 2.

To Figure 7 and Figure 8, an increase in number of segments means extra computations needed and this leads to an increase in elapsed time and CPU time in MATLAB for example 2.

Example 3

As example to the iterated integral, the following integral is presented [7].

$$\int_0^1 \int_0^1 \left(\left(\frac{1}{x+1} \right) + \left(\frac{1}{y+1} \right) \right) dxdy \tag{21}$$

The exact result of this integral is 1.386. The computation results and ε of related methods for $n \leq 5$ are presented in Table 9 and Table 10, respectively.

Table 9. Computation results of example 3 for $n \leq 5$

n	Methods	Results
2	Composite Trapezoidal Rule	1.4167
	Simpson's 1/3 Rule	1.3889
4	Composite Trapezoidal Rule	1.394
	Composite Simpson's 1/3 Rule	1.3865
5	Composite Trapezoidal Rule	1.3913
	Boole's rule	1.3863

Table 10. ε results of example 3 for $n \leq 5$

n	Methods	Results
2	Composite Trapezoidal Rule	2.1909
	Simpson's 1/3 Rule	0.1870
4	Composite Trapezoidal Rule	0.5593
	Composite Simpson's 1/3 Rule	0.01541
5	Composite Trapezoidal Rule	0.3589
	Boole's rule	0.002287

To Table 9 and Table 10, the calculations by Simpson's 1/3 rule, Composite Simpson's 1/3 rule and Boole's rule converge to the exact result of the problem more than Composite Trapezoidal method.

The elapsed time and CPU time in MATLAB for the related methods when $n \leq 5$ are presented in the Table 11 and Table 12 in terms of seconds, respectively.

Table 11. Elapsed time for computations of example 3 for $n \leq 5$

n	Methods	Results
2	Composite Trapezoidal Rule	0.01303
	Simpson's 1/3 Rule	0.01114
4	Composite Trapezoidal Rule	0.021055
	Composite Simpson's 1/3 Rule	0.3518
5	Composite Trapezoidal Rule	0.024532
	Boole's rule	0.01853

Table 12. CPU time for computations of example 3 for $n \leq 5$

n	Methods	Results
2	Composite Trapezoidal Rule	0.0000
	Simpson's 1/3 Rule	0.0156
4	Composite Trapezoidal Rule	0.0156
	Composite Simpson's 1/3 Rule	0.0468
5	Composite Trapezoidal Rule	0.0468
	Boole's rule	0.0000

To Table 11 and Table 12, the elapsed time for Simpson's 1/3 rule is the minimum whereas CPU time for Composite Trapezoidal rule (when n = 2) and Boole's rule (when n = 5) are minimum in Matlab for example 3.

The results of computation and error analysis of related methods for $n > 5$ are displayed in Figure 9 and Figure 10, respectively.

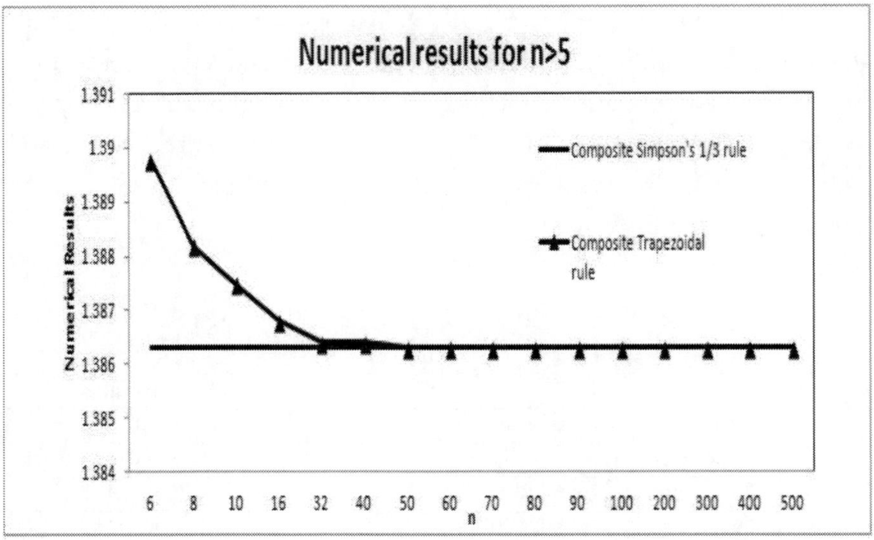

Figure 9. Computation results of example 3 for $n > 5$.

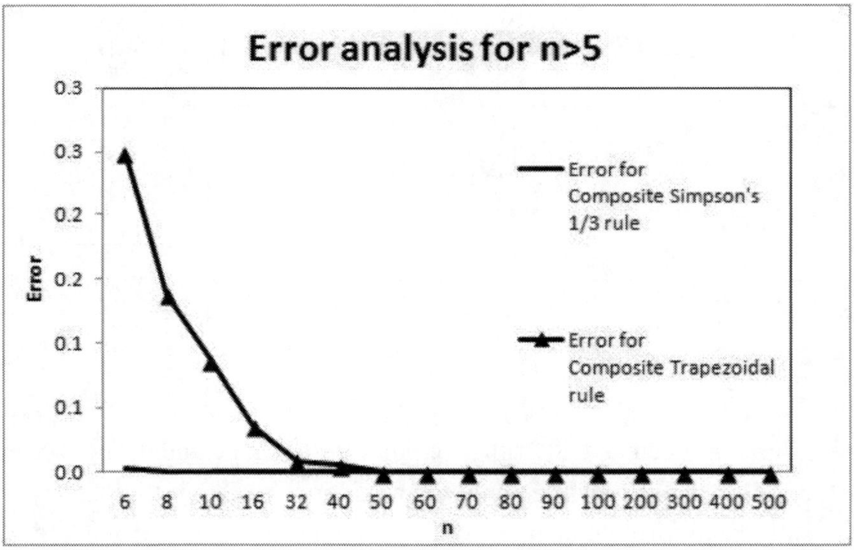

Figure 10. ε results of example 3 for n > 5.

To both Figure 9 and Figure 10, Composite Trapezoidal method gives more error. When n = 50, the exact result is computed by Composite Trapezoidal rule, simultaneously.

Elapsed time and CPU time for computation of all segments up to 500 segments are plotted in Figure 11 and Figure 12, respectively.

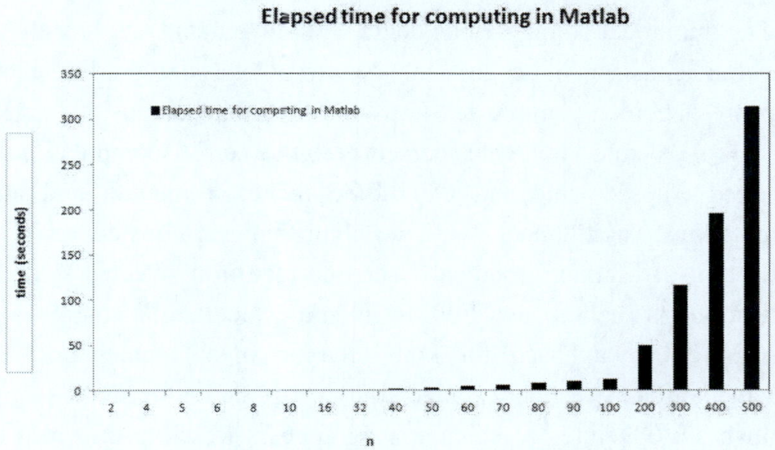

Figure 11. Elapsed time for computations (up to 500 segments) in example 3.

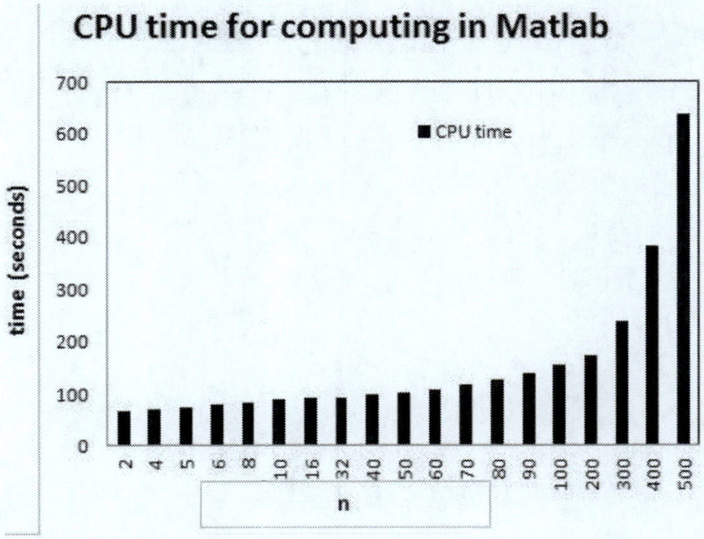

Figure 12. CPU time for computations (up to 500 segments) in example 3.

To Figure 11 and Figure 12, an increase in number of segments leads to an increase in elapsed time and CPU time in MATLAB for example 3.

TWOD_INTEGRAL_CALCULATOR AND IMPLEMENTATION

The numerical computations begin with developing an algorithm. This algorithm consists of codes for Newton-Cotes integration methods; Simpson's 1/3 rule, Composite Simpson's 1/3 rule, Composite Trapezoidal rule, Boole's rule and true percent relative error computations with measured elapsed time and CPU time for each method and also all computations, simultaneously. The algorithm is adjusted as a guide application of Matlab Graphical User Interface in a selected folder. This application is called as TWOD_integral_calculator. Matlab R2016a (9.0.0.341360) was used for both creation of this calculator and its implementation. Once, one enters the word 'guide' into the command window, TWOD_integral_calculator.fig appears which is shown in Figure 13.

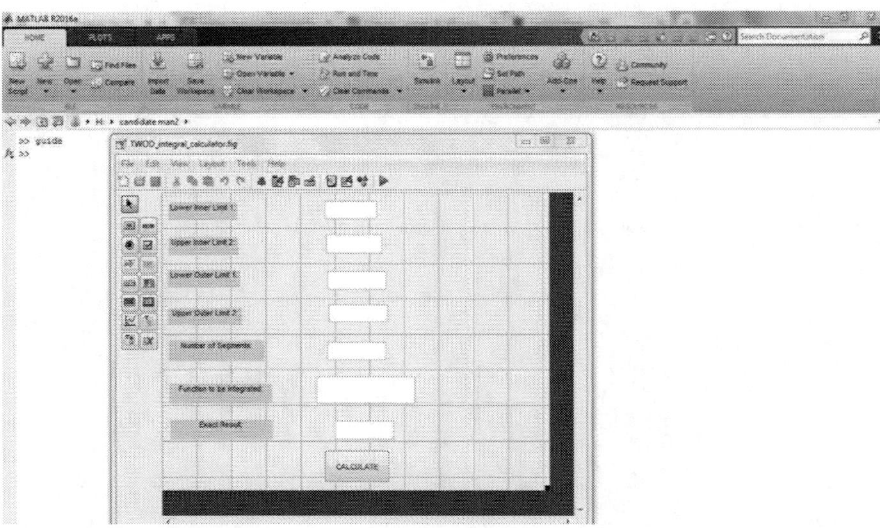

Figure 13. Display of TWOD_integral_calculator.fig.

This is the first image of the calculator. Seven input boxes are generated here. These boxes are 'Lower Inner Limit 1', 'Upper Inner Limit 2', 'Lower Outer Limit 1', 'Upper Outer Limit 2', 'Number of Segments', 'Function to be Integrated' and 'Exact Result'. 'CALCULATE' button is also generated. This button includes whole numerical integration algorithm of the TWOD_integral_calculator script file. This script file underlies TWOD_integral_calculator as GUI application.

The purpose is to make TWOD_integral_calculator be ready for computations. By entering 'TWOD_integral_calculator' into Matlab command window, final form of TWOD_integral_calculator can appear which is presented in Figure 14. It is waiting for the data entries.

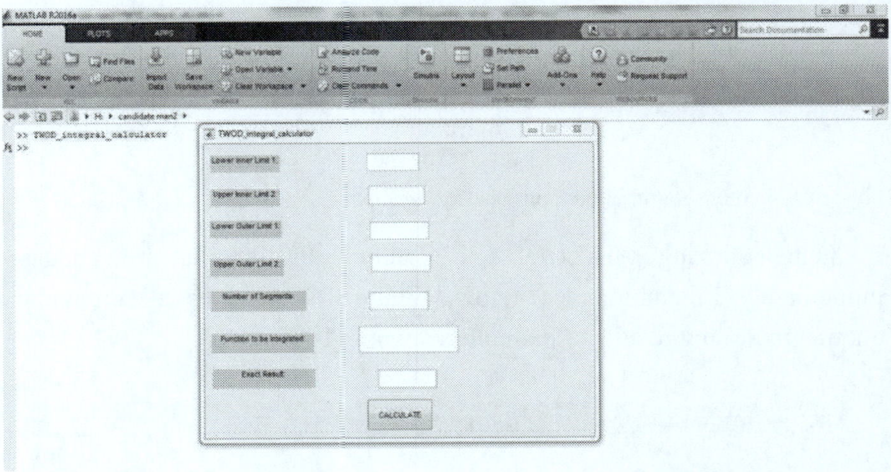

Figure 14. Final form of TWOD_integral_calculator.

TWOD_integral_calculator box requires 'Lower Inner Limit 1', 'Upper Inner Limit 2', 'Lower Outer Limit 1', 'Upper Outer Limit 2', 'Number of Segments', 'Function to be Integrated' and 'Exact Result' from user.

After filling out the boxes with 'Lower Inner Limit 1', 'Upper Inner Limit 2', 'Lower Outer Limit 1', 'Upper Outer Limit 2', 'Number of Segments', 'Function to be Integrated' and 'Exact Result' (if available) then computations start. As an illustration; the numerical data of the first example have been entered into the corresponding input boxes. The screenshot of this process is given in Figure 15.

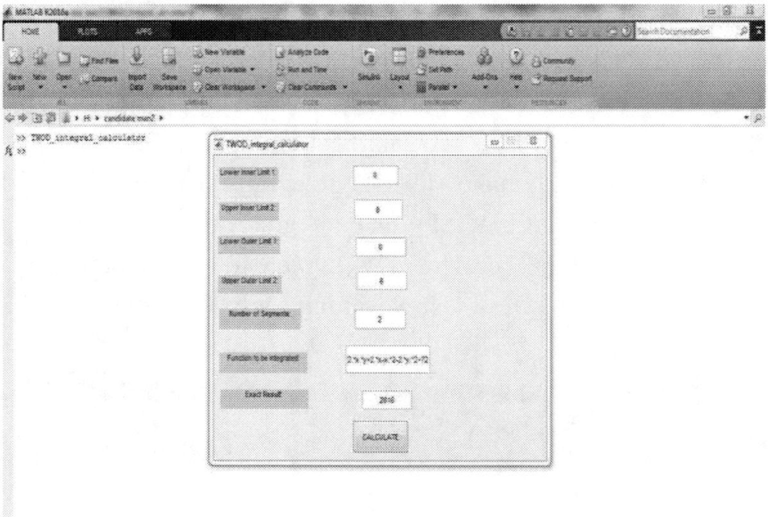

Figure 15. Screenshot of filled input box for example 1.

Once clicking 'CALCULATE' button, the results are appeared immediately in command window. Figure 16 indicates all inputs and outputs including results of example 1, explicitly.

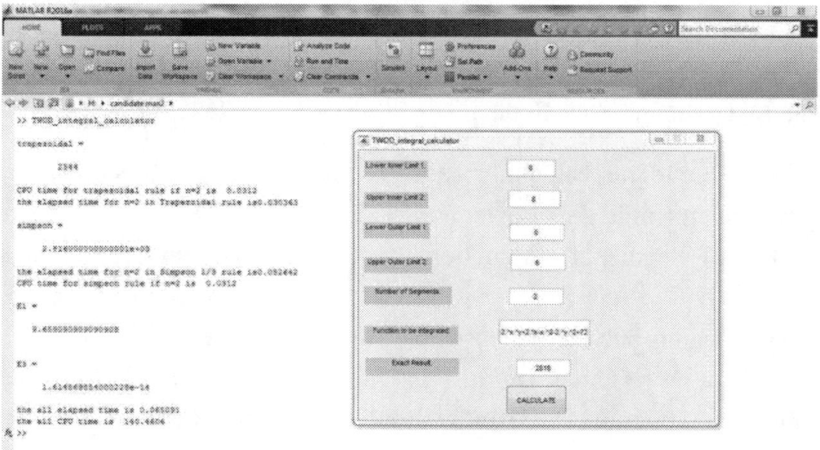

Figure 16. Display of both inputs and results of example 1.

Here, when n = 2 segments, user can obtain results from Composite Trapezoidal rule (named as 'trapezoidal') and Simpson's 1/3 rule (named as 'simpson') with corresponding true percent relative error represented as E1 and E3 for Composite Trapezoidal rule and Simpson's 1/3 rule, respectively. Elapsed time and CPU time for both Composite Trapezoidal rule and Simpson's 1/3 rule are also presented in Figure 16 for example 1.

Similarly, the numerical data of the second example have been entered into the related input boxes in TWOD_integral_calculator box. The screenshot of this process is given in Figure 17.

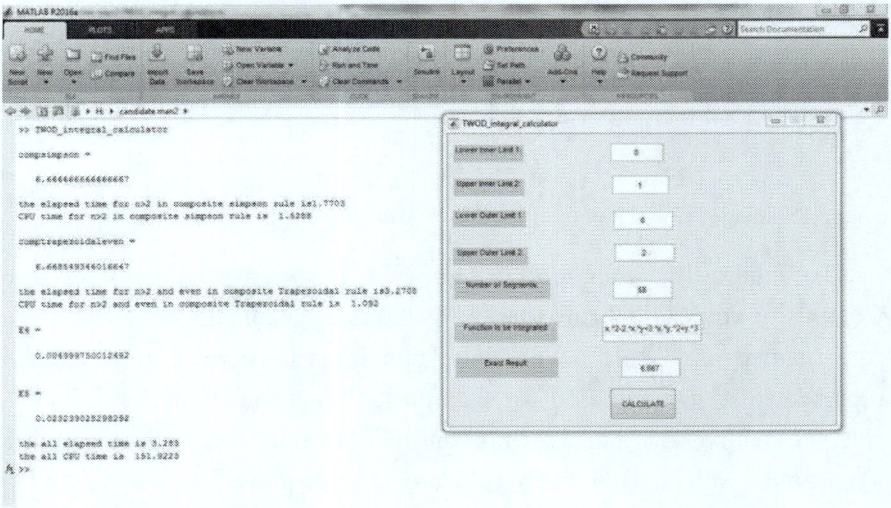

Figure 17. Display of both inputs and results of example 2.

Here, when n = 58 segments, user can obtain results from Composite Trapezoidal rule (named as 'comptrapezoidaleven') and Composite Simpson's 1/3 rule (named as 'compsimpson') with corresponding true percent relative error represented as E4 and E5 for Composite Simpson's 1/3 rule and Composite Trapezoidal rule, respectively. For example 2, elapsed time and CPU time for both Composite Trapezoidal rule and Composite Simpson's 1/3 rule are also shown in Figure 17.

Finally, the numerical data of the third example have been entered into the related input boxes in TWOD_integral_calculator box. The final image of this process is presented in Figure 18.

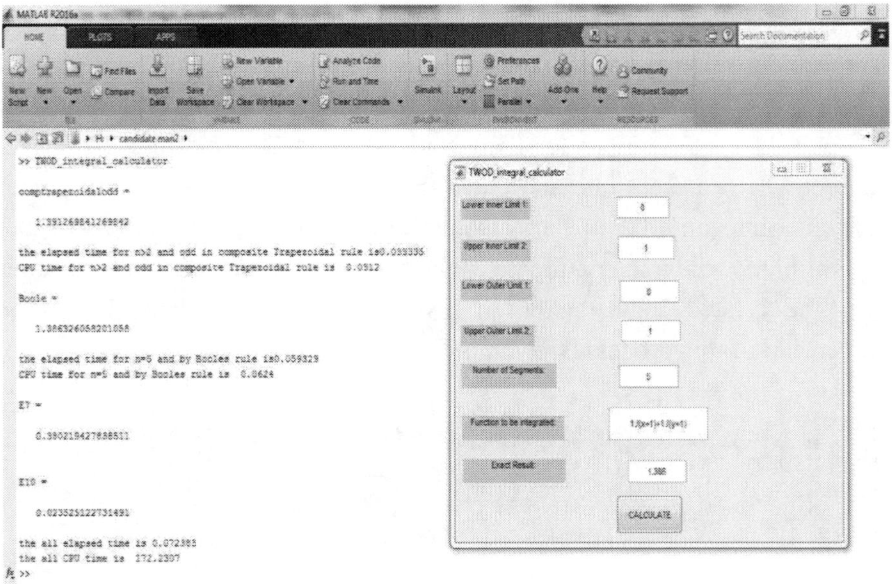

Figure 18. Image of both inputs and results of example 3.

To Figure 18, when n = 5 segments, user can obtain results from Composite Trapezoidal rule (named as 'comptrapezoidalodd') and Boole's rule (named as 'Boole') with corresponding true percent relative error represented as E7 and E10 for Composite Trapezoidal rule and Boole's rule, respectively. Elapsed time and CPU time for both Composite Trapezoidal rule and Boole's rule are also displayed in Figure 18 for example 3.

CONCLUSION

Most of the solutions for the problems in engineering and mathematics necessitate the solutions of nonlinear 2D integrals. If the function to be integrated is complicated, numerical computations such as Newton-Cotes integration methods (Simpson's 1/3, Composite Trapezoidal, Composite Simpson's 1/3, and Boole's rules) are employed to obtain the results. Since analytical result is the exact result in other words, true result. The application of Newton-Cotes integration methods into governing problem brings forward results which are convergent to the exact results. In order to obtain the closest result to the exact result, greater n values (number of segments) are required in many cases. All of these computations for each method require plenty of time, simultaneously.

In the light of these things above, this chapter mainly focused on design of a nonlinear 2D integral calculator (called as TWOD_integral_calculator) for the evaluation of nonlinear 2D integrals. TWOD_integral_calculator is designed by use of Matlab Graphical User Interface (GUI). This calculator is so user-friendly that any kind of users (educator, student) can employ it conveniently for any 2D integral given. It allows the user to obtain the integration results from each numerical integration method at the same time by entering lower limits, upper limits, number of segments, function to be integrated and exact result (if it is known).

The speed of this calculator in terms of elapsed and CPU time and convergence of these methods to the exact results in terms of true percent relative error are also computed for various numbers of segments. It is observed that use of Simpson's 1/3 rule, Composite Simpson's 1/3 rule and Boole's rule provides exact results in example 1 and example 2 and converges to exact result more successfully than Composite Trapezoidal method when n is less than and equal to five. In other words, an increase in number segments leads more computations to converge exact results, it is shown that use of small number of segments (in other words; $n \leq 5$) for Simpson's 1/3 and Composite Simpson's 1/3 rules is sufficient to obtain the exact results.

Composite Simpson's 1/3 rule is also more successful method than Composite Trapezoidal in terms of convergence to exact result in all examples when n is greater than five.

Furthermore, an increase in number of segments leads to an increase in both elapsed time and CPU time. TWOD_integral_calculator is practical in terms of less computational elapsed and CPU time.

This calculator is also a helpful calculator such that it can perform only numerical computations without true percent relative error calculations if one does not know the exact result of the integral.

REFERENCES

[1] Hammer, P. C., Wymore, A. W. (1957). Numerical evaluation of multiple integrals I, *Mathematical Tables and Other Aids to Computation*, 11: 59-67.

[2] Hammer, P. C., Stroud, A. H. (1958). Numerical evaluation of multiple integrals II, *Mathematical Tables and Other Aids to Computation*, 12: 272-280.

[3] Lether, F. G. (1976). Computation of 2D integrals over a triangle, *J. Comput. Appl. Math.,* 2: 219-224.

[4] Bentsen, J., Espelid, T. O., Genz, A. (1991). An Adaptive Algorithm for the Approximate Calculation of Multiple Integrals, *ACM Trans. Math. Softw.*, 17: 437-451.

[5] Carstairs, A. (1991). *Numerical Solutions to Two-Dimensional Integration Problems*, Mathematics Theses, Georgia State University, USA.

[6] Yeh, T. (1997). Trapezoidal rule for multiple integrals over hyperquadrilaterals, *Appl. Math. Comput.*, 87: 227-246.

[7] Edwards, C. H., Penny, D. E. (1999). *Calculus with Analytic Geometry*. Prentice Hall, Upper Saddle River NJ.

[8] Horwitz, A. (2001). A version of Simpson's rule for multiple integrals, *J. Comput. Appl. Math.,* 134:1-11.

[9] Li, Z. H., Zhang, H. X. (2004). Study on gas kinetic unified algorithm for flows from rarefied transition to Continuum, *J. Comput. Phys.*, 193: 708-738.

[10] Thong, Y. K., Woolfson, M. S., Crowe, J. A., Hayes-Gill, B. R. and Jones, D. A. (2004). Numerical double integration of acceleration measurements in noise, *Measurement,* 36:73-92.

[11] Sermutlu, E. (2005). Comparison of Newton–Cotes and Gaussian methods of quadrature, *Appl. Math. Comput.* 171:1048-1057.

[12] Tiraie, A. (2005). A Numerical Method for Solving 2D Integral Equations, Master's Theses, San Jose State University.

[13] Rathod, H.T., Nagaraja, K.V., Venkatesudu, B. (2007). On the application of two symmetric Gauss Legendre quadrature rules for composite numerical integration over a triangular surface, *Appl. Math. Comput.,* 190: 21-39.

[14] Chapra, S. C. Canale R. P. (2010). *Numerical Methods for Engineers.* McGraw-Hill, New York.

[15] Gao, X. W. (2010). An Effective Method for Numerical Evaluation of General 2D and 3D High Order Singular Boundary Integrals, *Comput. Methods Appl. Mech. Engrg.*, 199: 2856-2864.

[16] Gao, X. W. (2010). Numerical Evaluation of Two-Dimensional Singular Boundary Integrals-Theory and Fortran Code, *J. Comput. Appl. Math.*, 199: 2856-2864.

[17] Magalhaes, C. A. Junior, P. A. A. M. (2010). Higher-order-Newton-Cotes-Formulas, *Journal of Mathematics and Statistics*, 6: 193 204.

[18] Burden, R. L., Faires, J. D. (2011). *Numerical Analysis*, Brooks/Cole Cengage Learning, Boston.

[19] Islam, A. I., Khan, S. W. (2011). Quadrature rules for numerical integration based on Haar wavelets and hybrid functions, *Computers and Mathematics with Applications*, 61: 2770-2781.

[20] Li, J., Yu, D.-h. (2011). The Superconvergence of certain two-dimensional Cauchy principal value integrals, *CMES,* 71:331-346.

[21] Gasimova, N. F. (2012). Approximate solution for a class of two-dimensional nonlinear singular integral equations by the contraction mapping method, *Mathematical Notes*, 92:356-361.

[22] Jaluria, Y. (2012). *Computer Methods for Engineering with MATLAB Applications*. Taylor&Francis, New York.

[23] Ahmedov, A. A., Sathar, M. H. (2013). Numerical integration of the integrals based on Haar Wavelets, *Journal of Physics: Conference Series: Contemporary Mathematics, Mathematical Physics and their Application,* 435: 1-9.

[24] Altaç, Z., Tekkalmaz (2014). M. Radiative Transfer in Absorbing, Emitting and isotropically scattering segregated two-layered, 3D rectangular enclosures, *Journal of Quantitative Spectroscopy& Radiative Transfer*, 133: 570-578.

[25] Lin, H., Zhang, M., Mei, R., Chen, J., Hong, H. (2014). A novel approach for quantitative evaluation of the physicochemical interactions between rough membrane surface and sludge foulants in a submerged membrane bioreactor. *Bioresource Technol.*, 171: 247-252.

[26] Li, J., Zhaoa, Q., Huang, H. (2016). Error expansion of piecewise constant interpolation rule for certain two dimensional Cauchy principal value integrals, *Computers and Mathematics with Applications*, 72: 2119-2142.

[27] Linge, S., Langtangen, H. P. (2016). Programming for Computations. Matlab/Octave, *Texts in Computational Science and Engineering*, 14: 47-85.

[28] Mustafa, N. (2016). Newton-Kantorovich method for two-dimensional non-linear singular integral equations, *Maejo International Journal of Science and Technology*, 10: 41-50.

[29] Farshid, M., Elham, H. (2017). A new computational method for solving two-dimensional Stratonovich Volterra Integral Equation, *Mathematical Methods in the Applied Sciences*, 40: 5777-5791.

[30] Li J. Rui, H. (2017). Error expansion of trapezoidal rule for certain two- dimensional Cauchy principal value integrals, *Computers and Mathematics with Applications*, 74: 2608-2637.

INDEX

J

L

M

N

O

P